GRAMMAR IN PRACTICE

A Foundation

Lesli J. Favor, Ph.D.

her vs, hers Pg. 57

AMSCO

AMSCO SCHOOL PUBLICATIONS, INC.
315 HUDSON STREET, NEW YORK, N.Y. 10013

Cover Design: Meghan J. Shupe
Cover Art: iStockphoto.com/Stefan Junger
Text Design: Nesbitt Graphics, Inc.
Compositor: Nesbitt Graphics, Inc.

When ordering this book, please specify: *either* **R 017 W** *or*
GRAMMAR IN PRACTICE: A FOUNDATION

Please visit our Web site at: ***www.amscopub.com***

ISBN 978-1-56765-133-1
NYC Item 56765-133-0

Copyright © 2006 by Amsco School Publications, Inc.

PRINTED IN THE UNITED STATES OF AMERICA

6 7 8 9 10   10 09

About the Author

Lesli J. Favor loves grammar! She began her career in education as a writing tutor at the University of Texas at Arlington. After earning her BA in English there, she earned her MA and Ph.D. at the University of North Texas. While there, she taught courses in composition and literature. Afterward, she was assistant professor of English at Sul Ross State University-Rio Grande College. Now, as an educational writer, she is the author of fourteen books for young adult readers and students. She lives in the Seattle area with her husband, two dogs, and a horse.

Consultants

Nancy Mae Antrim is an assistant professor of English and Linguistics at Sul State University. Her Ph.D. is in linguistics from the University of Southern California. Prior to completing her doctorate, she taught ESL at Riverside High School in El Paso, Texas. Currently her teaching and research interests involve language teaching and methodology and second language acquisition. She has presented her research at numerous national and international conferences.

Linda Gonzales, Ph.D., earned her doctorate from The Claremont Graduate School and San Diego State University. Her undergraduate degree is from Chapman University. She also holds one master's degree in multicultural education and a second in public school administration. She has taught and worked at the elementary, middle school, and high school levels. She has also been an elementary school principal, an assistant and deputy superintendent, a superintendent, and director of state and federal projects.

Gary Pankiewicz has been teaching high school English for ten years at Hasbrouck Heights High School in Bergen County, New Jersey. He received his BA and MA (with a concentration in Composition Studies) from Montclair State University.

for Kathryn Rogers,
grammar goddess

Contents

Introduction: How to Use This Book—and Why vii

PART 1   THE EIGHT PARTS OF SPEECH_____ 1

Lesson 1   The Subject   2
Compound Subjects   9

Lesson 2   The Predicate   13

Lesson 3   Verbs   18 ✓
Action and Linking Verbs   20
Helping Verbs and Verb Phrases   25
Verbs in Contractions   29

Lesson 4   Compound Verbs   32 ✓

Lesson 5   Nouns   38
Common and Proper Nouns   41

Lesson 6   Nouns as Direct and Indirect Objects   46

Lesson 7   Pronouns and Antecedents   56 ✓
Personal Pronouns   59
Pronouns in Contractions   64

Lesson 8   Review of Verbs, Nouns, and Pronouns   67

Real-World Applications: Verbs, Nouns, and Pronouns   75

Lesson 9   Adjectives   77
Proper Adjectives   82
Predicate Adjectives and Predicate Nouns   86

Lesson 10   Adverbs   92 ✓
Forming Adverbs from Adjectives   97
Recognizing Adverbs and Adjectives   99

Lesson 11   Review of Adjectives and Adverbs   101

Lesson 12   Prepositions   107
Prepositional Phrases   110

Lesson 13   Conjunctions   116

Lesson 14   Interjections   122 ✓

Lesson 15   Review of Prepositions, Conjunctions,
and Interjections   125

[handwritten note near Lesson 3: Practice all types of verbs]

[handwritten note near Lesson 10: Review more!!]

Lesson 16   Review of the Eight Parts of Speech   131

Real-World Applications: Parts of Speech   135

Test Practice: Parts of Speech   137

PART 2   PUNCTUATION _____ 141

Lesson 17   End Punctuation   142

Lesson 18   The Comma   144

Lesson 19   The Semicolon and the Colon   148

Lesson 20   The Apostrophe   153

Lesson 21   Quotation Marks   156

Lesson 22   Punctuating Titles   161

Lesson 23   Review of Punctuation   163

Real-World Applications: Punctuation   168

Test Practice: Punctuation   170

PART 3   CAPITALIZATION _____ 173

Lesson 24   Helpful Capitalization Rules   174

Lesson 25   Review of Capitalization   181

Real-World Applications: Capitalization   184

Test Practice: Capitalization   186

PART 4   SPELLING _____ 189

Lesson 26   Helpful Spelling Rules   190

Lesson 27   Plural Nouns   197

Lesson 28   Review of Spelling   207

Real-World Applications: Spelling   211

Test Practice: Spelling   213

Test Practice: Parts of Speech, Punctuation, Capitalization, Spelling   216

Glossary   *219*
Index   *221*

INTRODUCTION
How to Use This Book
—and Why

A thorough understanding of grammar and the mechanics of writing is one of the pillars of a solid education. It prepares you for success in college, careers, and daily life. For this reason, now more than ever, students are being asked to demonstrate proficiency in grammar, usage, and composition. State tests, the SAT, and the ACT will measure your ability to recognize and correct errors in grammar and mechanics. These tests as well as your classroom assignments require that you write clear, correct sentences and paragraphs, both in isolation and in essay format.

This is the first in a series of books that offers instruction, review, and practice in the basics of grammar, mechanics, and composition. The concepts build on one another, from the parts of speech through paragraph composition, so that when you complete the final book, you will have the tools necessary to assemble polished compositions. Specifically, this book covers the parts of speech, grammar rules, punctuation, capitalization, and spelling. *Grammar in Practice: Usage* offers expanded instruction on grammar, common usage errors, and using different kinds of sentences. *Grammar in Practice: Sentences and Paragraphs,* shows you how to pull together your grammar and usage skills to write strong, engaging sentences and paragraphs.

Here in *Grammar in Practice: A Foundation* you will find a variety of lessons, features, and activities:

- **Instructional sections:** Short, easy to read sections introduce and explain key concepts, complete with definitions, explanations, and examples. Your teacher may skip sections you already know well and return for review to sections that were especially helpful or important.

- **Activities:** Many brief workbook-style exercises let you practice applying lesson concepts. Literature-based exercises require critical analysis of specific points of grammar, mechanics, or style in an excerpt.

- **Composition Hints:** These features offer tips and techniques for applying rules and for developing your personal style in writing.

- **ESL Focus:** These features explain points of grammar and usage that can be particularly challenging to non-native English speakers.

- **Writing Applications:** To help you integrate the grammar and usage concepts you learn, you'll often be asked to write and revise sentences and paragraphs, occasionally working with a classmate.

- **Games and Puzzles:** Throughout the book you will find crossword puzzles, word-seek puzzles, word jumbles, and other word games that will reinforce what you're learning. They offer a fun yet challenging way to approach grammar. Depending on the puzzle, your teacher may have you work in pairs or may provide hints or word lists derived from the teacher's manual.

- **Real-World Applications:** These assignments at the end of each lesson group let you explore how people use grammar, mechanics, and sentences in the real world, outside classroom walls. With them, you'll have the opportunity to showcase your strengths while incorporating your individual style and creativity. Many of them feature technology applications.

- **Test Practice:** Each lesson group concludes with a practice test covering only the material in those lessons. Additionally, the book concludes with a comprehensive test covering major concepts in the book. Most tests are multiple choice and are modeled after state-proficiency and standardized tests you will take in order to graduate or apply to colleges.

With so much variety, this book is an invaluable tool. Your teacher can pick and choose lessons, work through from beginning to end, or have you use the book as a homework resource. However you and your teacher decide to use it, you'll find your skills in grammar and mechanics growing sharper. Continue with the rest of the series, and you will be able to write interesting and effective compositions with confidence and flair.

Lesli J. Favor, Ph.D.
Author

Auditi Chakravarty
Editor

The Eight Parts of Speech

In a sentence, a word may play one of eight parts. It may be

- a noun
- a pronoun
- a verb
- an adjective

- an adverb
- a preposition
- a conjunction
- an interjection

 These eight parts are known as the parts of speech.

We use the parts of speech to build sentences. For example, if we put together the noun *friendship* and the verb *lasts*, we can make the following statement:

Friendship lasts.
 N.   V.

We can expand this statement by adding the adjective *true*.

True friendship lasts.
ADJ.   N.   V.

We can also add the adverb *forever*.

True friendship lasts *forever*.
ADJ.   N.   V.   ADV.

If we want to ask a question, we can begin with a verb. Here is a question made up of the verb *is*, the noun *friendship*, and the adverb *forever*.

Is friendship forever?
V.   N.   ADV.

Of course, we can expand this question. For example, we can add the possessive pronoun *our*.

Is *our* friendship forever?
V. PRO.   N.   ADV.

We can respond to the question *Is our friendship forever?* using all eight parts of speech, including an interjection and a conjunction.

Of course! True friendship lasts, and ours is forever.
INTER.   ADJ.   N.   V.   CONJ. PRO. V.   ADV.

 The system that our language uses to put parts of speech together into sentences is known as *grammar*.

The first two lessons in Part One focus on the two basic parts of any sentence: the *subject* and the *predicate*.

1

The Subject

A sentence has two parts: (1) a *subject* and (2) a *predicate*. This lesson deals with the subject.

 The *subject* is the part of the sentence about which something is told or asked.

The California gold rush began in 1848.

    QUESTION: About what is the sentence telling something?

    ANSWER: *The California gold rush*

    SUBJECT: *The California gold rush*

James Marshall discovered gold at Sutter's Mill.

    QUESTION: About whom is the sentence telling something?

    ANSWER: *James Marshall*

    SUBJECT: *James Marshall*

Do gold nuggets sparkle in the sunlight?

    QUESTION: About what is the sentence asking something?

    ANSWER: *gold nuggets*

    SUBJECT: *gold nuggets*

QUESTION: Why should I know how to identify the subject of a sentence?

ANSWER: The subject is one of the two main building blocks of a sentence (the other is the predicate, covered in Lesson 2). Being able to identify the subject helps you understand and follow many rules of grammar. Also, you are better able to write different kinds of sentences, including those with compound subjects. (More about compound subjects later.)

ACTIVITY 1

Write the subject of each sentence.

> **Samples:**
>
> **a.** A pride of lions rested in the shade.
>
> *About what is this sentence saying something?*   A pride of lions
>
> **b.** Does anyone on the bus have two quarters?
>
> *About what is this sentence asking something?* anyone on the bus

1. The pack of colored markers costs two dollars.

   About what is this sentence saying something?   _____

2. Someone with muddy boots messed up the floor.

About whom is this sentence saying something? _____

3. Does this green necktie match my shirt?

About what is this sentence asking something? _____

4. Last year's fashions are priced affordably.

About what is this sentence saying something? _____

5. Will Tina Ellis remember her promise?

About whom is this sentence asking something? _____

QUESTION: Where is the subject usually found in a sentence?

ANSWER: The subject is usually found at the beginning of the sentence, but it can also appear in other positions.

BEGINNING: *John Sutter* was building a sawmill.

MIDDLE: One morning, *Sutter's employee* spotted gold in the river.

END: On the banks of the river was *Sutter's Mill*.

A sure way to find the subject is to answer one or the other of these questions:
- About whom or what is the sentence saying or asking something?
- Who or what is doing, or has done, or will do something?

EXAMPLE 1

What is the subject of the following sentence?

Gold nuggets sparkled in the American River.

QUESTION: About what is the sentence saying something?

ANSWER: The sentence is saying something about *Gold nuggets.*

SUBJECT: *Gold nuggets*

This subject tells *about what* the sentence is saying something.

EXAMPLE 2

What is the subject of the following sentence?

A curious James Marshall waded in and scooped them up.

QUESTION: Who did something?

ANSWER: A curious James Marshall did something.

SUBJECT: *A curious James Marshall*

This subject tells *who* did something.

EXAMPLE 3

What is the subject of the following sentence?

Keep our gold mine a secret.

QUESTION: Who is to do something?

ANSWER: <u>You</u> (understood) are to do something (*You* keep our gold mine a secret).

SUBJECT: *you* (understood)

Note: In an *imperative sentence* (a sentence expressing a command or making a request), the subject *You* may not be stated but is understood.

EXAMPLE 4

What is the subject of the following sentence?

Did the secret leak out anyway?

QUESTION: About what is the sentence asking?

ANSWER: The sentence is asking about <u>the secret.</u>

SUBJECT: *the secret*

This subject tells *about what* the sentence is asking.

ACTIVITY 2 ———————————————————————

Underline the subject in each sentence. If the subject is the understood *You*, write *You* on the line provided. The first five sentences give you hints to help identify each subject.

> **Samples:**
>
> _____ **a.** Did <u>the lucky John Sutter</u> become rich from his gold mine? (*Who did something?*)
>
> __You__ **b.** Help me pan for gold, please. (*Who is to do something?*)

_____ **1.** News of Sutter's gold spread as quickly as wildfire. (*About what is the sentence saying something?*)

_____ **2.** Like a greedy river, prospectors flooded Sutter's land. (*Who did something?*)

_____ **3.** Keep away from my gold mine! (*Who is to do something?*)

_____ **4.** The thought of great riches was irresistible. (*About what is the sentence saying something?*)

_____ **5.** At the heart of everyone's fantasies was easy riches. (*About what is the sentence saying something?*)

_____ **6.** Sutter's own employees panned for gold.

_____ **7.** Unfortunately, the gold seekers stole freely from Sutter.

_____ **8.** Besides that, the landowner had little business sense.

_____ **9.** Does this story have a happy ending?

_____ **10.** Eventually, Sutter lost his land and died poor.

Writing Application

Using Subjects in Sentences

Like the gold seekers at Sutter's Mill, many people value riches. If you listed the five things you value most, would riches be on the list?

On a separate sheet of paper, write **five** sentences about the **five** things you value most. Underline the subject in each sentence. Here is an example: <u>Good grades</u> are important to me. Try writing at least one sentence in which the subject appears in the middle or at the end of the sentence.

Simple Subject and Complete Subject

Until now, we have focused on the *complete subject* of a sentence. The main word or word group in the complete subject is called the *simple subject*. The other words in the complete subject help describe the simple subject. Usually, when people talk about the subject of a sentence, they mean the simple subject.

 When a subject consists of more than one word, the main word in that subject is called the *simple subject*.

My favorite *author* is Lois Lowry.

> COMPLETE SUBJECT: My favorite author

> SIMPLE SUBJECT: *author*

The amazing *Lois Lowry* is my favorite author.

> COMPLETE SUBJECT: The amazing Lois Lowry

> SIMPLE SUBJECT: *Lois Lowry*

ACTIVITY 3

In each sentence, the complete subject is underlined. Write the simple subject on the line provided.

> **Sample:**
>
> _____*cans*_____ **a.** The empty aluminum cans belong in the recycling bin.

_____ **1.** Paper plates are wasteful.

_____ **2.** Are clean, empty glass bottles recyclable?

_____ **3.** In that cupboard are several empty yogurt cups.

_____ **4.** These old, faded newspapers are gathering dust.

_____ **5.** In this house, the family's motto is, "Reduce, Reuse, Recycle."

As you can see in Sentences 1-5 above, the simple subject may be described by other words in a sentence. For example, in *Paper plates are wasteful,* the simple subject *plates* is described by the word *Paper.*

 The simple subject and the words that describe it are together known as the *complete subject.*

My favorite author is Lois Lowry.

> COMPLETE SUBJECT: My favorite author

QUESTION: Does a simple subject ever consist of more than one word?

ANSWER: Yes, especially if it is a name.

EXAMPLE: The funny Christopher Paul Curtis wrote *Bud, Not Buddy*.

> COMPLETE SUBJECT: The funny Christopher Paul Curtis

> SIMPLE SUBJECT: *Christopher Paul Curtis*

The simple subject is the key idea in the sentence. Without the simple subject, the sentence does not make sense, or it loses its key idea. You can test this. Take the sentence about Christopher Paul Curtis, for example. Try reading it without the simple subject.

The funny wrote *Bud, Not Buddy*.

Without *Christopher Paul Curtis,* the sentence makes no sense. This test proves *Christopher Paul Curtis* is the simple subject.

ACTIVITY 4

In each sentence, underline the complete subject. Then circle the simple subject.

> **Samples:**
>
> **a.** At the library are <u>many fascinating (books)</u>
>
> **b.** Is <u>the (magazine) in that rack</u> about fashion?

Hint: *To be sure you have correctly identified the simple subject, read the sentence* <u>without</u> *that word or those words. If the sentence no longer makes sense, you have correctly identified the simple subject.*

1. The volumes on that shelf are award winners.

2. Did your best friend read *Everything on a Waffle*?

3. Jared's main interest is sports stories.

4. In that display are the most popular novels.

5. Over there, librarian Rachel Fritz is reshelving biographies.

ACTIVITY 5

Complete each sentence by writing a simple subject on the *simple subject* line. Then use additional words to write a complete subject on the *complete subject* line.

> **Samples:**
>
> **a. 1.** _____Laughter_____ rang out during the funny movie.
> SIMPLE SUBJECT
>
> **2.** ___Sudden, loud laughter___ rang out during the funny movie.
> COMPLETE SUBJECT
>
> **b. 1.** At the bottom of the box were _____coins_____ .
> SIMPLE SUBJECT
>
> **2.** At the bottom of the box were ___several valuable coins___ .
> COMPLETE SUBJECT

1. a. _____ swung the bat at the baseball.
SIMPLE SUBJECT

b. _____ swung the bat at the baseball.
COMPLETE SUBJECT

2. a. After all that, _____ ate the new goldfish.
　　　　　　　　　SIMPLE SUBJECT

b. After all that, _____ ate the new goldfish.
　　　　　　　　COMPLETE SUBJECT

3. a. Behind the bushes were _____.
　　　　　　　　　　　　SIMPLE SUBJECT

b. Behind the bushes were _____.
　　　　　　　　　　　COMPLETE SUBJECT

4. a. _____ filled the sky.
　　　　　SIMPLE SUBJECT

b. _____ filled the sky.
　　　　COMPLETE SUBJECT

5. a. Did _____ remember your birthday?
　　　　　　　SIMPLE SUBJECT

b. Did _____ remember your birthday?
　　　　　COMPLETE SUBJECT

Writing Application

Using Simple Subjects and Complete Subjects in Sentences

In John Sutter's day (the mid-1800s), people struck gold by literally finding gold in the ground. How do people "strike gold" today? Write a paragraph of at least **five** sentences describing one or more ways people can strike it rich. In each sentence, underline the complete subject once, and circle the simple subject.

ACTIVITY 6

Underline the simple subject in each sentence. Then, in the puzzle, find the simple subject and circle it. Words may be embedded frontward, backward, up, down, or diagonally. One item is completed for you.

Sample:

In the rain forest, the flying <u>gecko</u> lives in trees.

1. This little lizard is a fantastic climber.

2. Its scaly feet can cling to slippery surfaces.

3. In trees, sharp claws on the feet grip bark.

4. The reptile's tail is about the same length as its body.

5. Oddly enough, this body part can break off.

6. Then, it slowly grows back.

7. The lizard's tongue licks its eyes clean.

8. The animal's eggs are soft and sticky at first.

9. Gradually the shells harden.

10. A baby breaks out of its shell with its "egg tooth."

Compound Subjects

 A *compound subject* consists of two or more subjects of the same verb connected by *and* or *or*.

Courtney *and* Vince grilled the steaks.
COMPOUND SUBJECT   VERB

Courtney is a subject of the verb *grilled*.

Vince is also a subject of the verb *grilled*.

These two subjects of the same verb, connected by *and*, are the compound subject *Courtney and Vince*.

A compound subject can consist of more than two subjects.

Steak, chicken, *or* pasta will be served at the banquet.

Steak is a subject of the verb *will be served*.

So, too, are *chicken* and *pasta*.

These three subjects of the same verb, connected by *or*, are the compound subject *Steak, chicken,* or *pasta*.

ACTIVITY 7

Underline the compound subject in each sentence. Then circle the connecting word.

> **Sample:**
>
> At the water's edge, <u>canoes, rafts,</u> (and) <u>boats</u> were stored.

1. Tents and campfires marked the campground.

2. Did Phillip, Todd, or LaVonn go fishing?

3. You or I must build the campfire.

4. Tonight, potatoes, apples, and marshmallows will be roasted.

5. By noon, rain and wind struck the camp.

Notice that when there are more than two subjects in a compound subject, a comma is placed after each one except the last.

Steak, chicken, or pasta will be served at the banquet.

Each subject in a compound subject may be modified by other words. Do not be distracted by these other words when you identify the parts of the compound subject.

A fat gray *cat* and a skinny orange *kitten* arrived on my doorstep.

(The compound subject is *cat and kitten*.)

The frail old *man* or his older, frailer *father* should have the bus seat.

(The compound subject is *man or father*.)

ACTIVITY 8

Write the compound subject of each sentence on the line provided.

> **Sample:**
>
> The wrinkled, dirty dollars and the shiny coins are all mine.
>
> _____ *dollars and coins* _____

1. Bratty little sisters and annoying little brothers are beloved, nevertheless.

_____

2. Red paint, loud mufflers, and a tree-shaped air freshener characterize the car.

_____

3. Are these old plastic chairs or the rusty metal bench Kim's?

_____

4. Skilled surfers, strong swimmers, and certified lifeguards love this beach.

_____

5. Does cheesy macaroni or a warm sandwich sound better?

_____

ACTIVITY 9 _____

Two five-letter nouns are hidden *backward* in each line. Some words may overlap by one letter. Find the twenty nouns and write them on the lines provided. Then write ten sentences using the ten pairs of nouns as compound subjects. A sample line is completed for you.

```
        tulip              G T P I L U T P A F O Y S I A D R R A D      daisy
 1. _____            U W S I Q U R Y M E N E C E I N M C O B    _____
 2. _____            N O O P S L O E J T Z S A E F I N K Y H    _____
 3. _____            A A R L S E T O N O H S A R T T M L O V    _____
 4. _____            I F Y H U B K R E L C P E Z A E G D U J    _____
 5. _____            N U K Y S K C O S T O O B E K G D O F I    _____
 6. _____            P T S I R W E Q Y H A W O B L E Z U U W    _____
 7. _____            O C U K Y N N E P J C I D V E S R U P A    _____
 8. _____            A L L R I A H C E L B A T T C E Y N O M    _____
 9. _____            H O P N N E L I M S Z I H G U A L I Q H    _____
10. _____            B U E K A N S I G E S U O M E F K C A C    _____
```

Sample:

A red tulip and a white daisy were in the bouquet.

11. _____

12. _____

13. _____

14. _____

15. _____

16. _____

17. _____

18. _____

19. _____

20. _____

Composition Hint

Compound subjects let us express ourselves in fewer words and without repetition. Consider this sentence:

Rain, snow, or sleet is expected by morning.

If there were no compound subjects, we would have to say

Rain is expected by morning. Snow is expected by morning. Sleet is expected by morning.

ACTIVITY 10

Express the following in fewer words by using a compound subject.

Sample:

Oklahoma borders Texas.   _Oklahoma and New Mexico_

New Mexico borders Texas.   _border Texas._

1. Shirts must be worn.   _____

    Shoes must be worn.   _____

2. Emily may hit a home run.   _____

    Ajay may hit a home run.   _____

3. Finally, the bus arrived.   _____

    Finally, the driver arrived. _____

4. Are hurricanes frightening? _____

    Are tornadoes frightening? _____

    Are floods frightening?   _____

5. Yes, teachers will be there. _____

    Yes, parents will be there. _____

    Yes, students will be there. _____

LESSON 2 The Predicate

As you learned in Lesson 1, the *subject* is the part of the sentence about which something is told or asked.

<u>Bees</u> make honey.
SUBJECT

Being able to identify the subject of a sentence helps you follow the rules of grammar and write clear, correct sentences. Just as important is the ability to identify the *predicate* of a sentence.

 The predicate is the part of the sentence that tells or asks something about the subject.

Bees <u>make honey</u>.
PREDICATE

You can easily find the subject and the predicate of a sentence by asking two simple questions:

TO FIND THE SUBJECT: About what or whom is the sentence telling or asking something?

TO FIND THE PREDICATE: What is the sentence saying or asking about the subject?

EXAMPLE 1

Bees make honey.

QUESTION: About what is the sentence telling something?

ANSWER: *Bees*

The subject is <u>Bees</u>.

QUESTION: What is the sentence saying about *Bees*?

ANSWER: *make honey.*

The predicate is <u>*make honey*</u>.

EXAMPLE 2

Teena's uncle Josh is running a marathon.

QUESTION: About whom is the sentence telling something?

ANSWER: *Teena's uncle Josh . . .*

The subject is <u>*Teena's uncle Josh*</u>.

QUESTION: What is the sentence saying about *Teena's uncle Josh*?

ANSWER: *. . . is running a marathon.*

The predicate is <u>is running a marathon</u>.

EXAMPLE 3

Was the party a surprise?

    QUESTION: About what is the sentence asking something?

    ANSWER: *. . . the party . . .*

           The subject is *the party*.

    QUESTION: What is the sentence asking about *the party?*

    ANSWER: *Was . . . a surprise?*

           The predicate is <u>Was a surprise</u>.

ACTIVITY 1

Write the predicate in each sentence.

> **Samples:**
>
> **a.** White chickens pecked at yellow grain.
>
> *What is the sentence saying about <u>white chickens</u>?* They <u>pecked at yellow</u>
>
> <u>grain.</u>
>
> **b.** Has Dad signed the permission slip?
>
> *What is the sentence saying about <u>Dad</u>?* Dad <u>has signed the permission slip.</u>

1. That hinge needs oil.

    What is the sentence saying about That hinge? It _____

2. Frida Kahlo married Diego Rivera.

    What is the sentence saying about Frida Kahlo? She _____

3. Marshmallows roasted over the fire.

    What is the sentence saying about Marshmallows? They _____

4. Has the cat eaten this morning?

    What is the sentence saying about the cat? The cat _____

5. A big storm is headed our way.

    What is the sentence saying about A big storm? It _____

Position of the Predicate

The predicate usually comes after the subject, but it can also appear in other positions.

The skateboarder <u>zoomed down the hill</u>.
    s.   P.

PREDICATE BEFORE THE SUBJECT

<u>Down the hill zoomed</u> the skateboarder.
    P.   S.

PREDICATE PARTLY BEFORE AND PARTLY AFTER THE SUBJECT

<u>Did</u> the skateboarder <u>zoom down the hill</u>?
 P.   S.   P.

ACTIVITY 2

First draw a single line under the complete subject of the sentence. Then write the predicate on the double line at the right. (*Hint: All words that are not in the complete subject are in the predicate.*)

Samples:

	SUBJECT	PREDICATE
a.	<u>The family</u> celebrated my birthday.	celebrated my birthday
b.	How difficult <u>that driver's test</u> was!	How difficult . . . was
c.	In the junkyard sat <u>my first car</u>.	In the junkyard sat

1. With his tools, Jordan repaired the car. _____

2. The hard work took many months. _____

3. Would you hand me that wrench? _____

4. Beside the house is the family's parking spot. _____

5. That modest, compact car is his life! _____

ACTIVITY 3

Complete each sentence by adding a predicate. Be sure to include a period at the end of the sentence, if needed.

Samples:

a. The strange yellow food _____ was our lunch. _____

b. _____ In the fifth row sat _____ an angry spectator.

1. The rock star _____

2. My worst enemy _____

3. _____ red lava and gray ash.

4. That fierce dragon _____

5. Your secret _____

6. _____ the employee of the month.

7. My sister Estella _____.

8. Harold's prize-winning pig _____

9. _____ a sticky wad of chewing gum.

10. _____ Professor Martinez.

ACTIVITY 4

Some parts of the following poem are underlined and numbered. Decide whether each underlined part is a subject or a predicate. On the line provided, write *subject* or *predicate*. Two items are completed for you.

The Arrow and the Song
Henry Wadsworth Longfellow

I shot an arrow into the air,   _____predicate_____
      (1)

It fell to earth, I know not where;   _____
(2)

For, so swiftly it flew, the sight   _____
        (3)

Could not follow it in its flight.

I breathed a song into the air,   _____
(4)

It fell to earth, I knew not where;   _____
    (5)

For who has sight so keen and strong,   _____
   (6)

That it can follow the flight of song?

Long, long afterward, in an oak   _____predicate_____

I found the arrow, still unbroke;
     (7)

And the song, from beginning to end,

I found again in the heart of a friend.

Writing Application

Using Predicates in Sentences

In "The Arrow and the Song," what do you think the speaker means when he says he "breathed a song into the air" and later found the song "in the heart of a friend"?

On a separate sheet of paper, write a paragraph of at least **five** sentences explaining your interpretation of this part of the poem. In each sentence, underline the predicate.

3 Verbs

 The main word in the predicate is called the *verb*.

Here are a few examples:

The band *practices* faithfully.

> PREDICATE: practices faithfully
>
> VERB: practices

Ramón often writes lyrics for the band's original songs.

> PREDICATE: often writes lyrics for the band's original songs
>
> VERB: writes

Are Ramón's songs good?

> PREDICATE: Are . . . good
>
> VERB: Are

Without a verb, the predicate cannot tell or ask anything about the subject. For instance, if the verb *practices* is left out of the first sentence above, the resulting sentence cannot convey any clear meaning.

The band faithfully.

ACTIVITY 1

Underline the predicate in each sentence. Then circle the verb.

> **Samples:**
>
> **a.** The rules of hygiene (govern) every teen's life.
>
> **b.** (Are) these rules reasonable?
>
> **c.** (Listen) to a few of these numerous commandments.

1. Every young man (shaves) his face daily.

2. (Brush) your teeth faithfully every morning.

3. (Is) that bar of soap just a suggestion?

4. Well-groomed women (regularly) wash their hair.

5. All of us (break) these rules sometimes.

QUESTION: Does a verb ever consist of more than one word?

ANSWER: Yes, often. A verb may consist of one to four words.

SENTENCE	VERB
Dana stepped in gum.	stepped
Did you spill this green paint?	Did spill
Josh has been dropping crumbs everywhere.	has been dropping
These messes could have been avoided.	could have been avoided

Not is never part of the verb. It is an *adverb*. (You will learn about adverbs in Lesson 10.)

ACTIVITY 2

Underline the predicate in each sentence. Then, on the line provided, write the verb.

Samples:

a. Global warming has become a serious issue. _____has become_____

b. Have these problems been reported in the news? __Have been reported__

1. Canadian red foxes have moved north. _have moved_

2. Some bird species now migrate four days earlier in the spring. _migrate_

3. Life-forms may have been affected worldwide. _have been affected_

4. Did the temperatures reach record highs last summer? _did...reach_

5. Certain plants may have unfolded their leaves days earlier than in the past. _have unfolded_

ACTIVITY 3

Underline the verb in each sentence. Then, on the line provided, use the same verb in a sentence of your own.

Sample:

You have been whispering about me all day.

Eva's friends have been whispering to one another.

1. Who shouted at the puppy?

   _____

2. With anger, the store owner was watching a shoplifter.

   _____

3. You have been nominated for the MVP award!

_____

4. Actually, the accident may have been caused by me.

_____

5. Has someone been repairing the back fence?

_____

Action and Linking Verbs

Verbs are grouped into two categories: *action verbs* and *linking verbs*. Being able to recognize and use each type of verb helps you write sentences that express ideas with precision and grammatical correctness.

An *action verb* expresses action.

As the label "action verb" suggests, all verbs in this category express some form of action. You may think immediately of physical action—singing, dancing, speaking, sneezing, walking, and so on. But don't forget that action verbs include those that express actions you cannot see—that is, mental action.

Active verbs

Physical action can be seen or heard.

The clown *stumbled, sat* on the cake, and *laughed* with glee.

(*Stumbled, sat,* and *laughed* express physical action.)

Mental action takes place in the mind and therefore cannot be seen or heard.

Officer Balkhi *thought* she *knew* who *planned* the crime.

(*Thought, knew,* and *planned* express mental action.)

ACTIVITY 4 _____

If the italicized verb expresses physical action, write P on the line provided. If it expresses mental action, write M.

> **Samples:**
>
> __M__ **a.** For days, I *memorized* lists of names and dates.
>
> __P__ **b.** I *carried* that heavy history book with me everywhere.

__P__ **1.** Sandra *had made* a stack of flash cards.

__M__ **2.** I *am studying* them along with her.

_P_ **3.** *Hand* me that page of notes, please.

_M_ **4.** Freddy *peeked* at my answers during the exam.

_M_ **5.** Who *thought* the history midterm was easy?

Writing Application

Using Action Verbs

Habits are simply actions that we repeat over and over. What habits do you have?

On a separate sheet of paper, write **five** sentences telling about five habits you have. Include at least one mental action. In each sentence, underline the action verb. Here is an example: I habitually <u>forget</u> my homework assignments.

Not all verbs are action verbs. The verb *is* in the following sentence does not express action. It is a *linking verb*.

Morgan <u>is</u> older than I.
    L.V.

The verb *is* has little meaning of its own. Its main function is to *link* (connect) *Morgan* with *older*. For this reason, we call *is* a **linking verb.**

 A *linking verb* links (connects) the subject with a word in the predicate that describes or identifies the subject.

That lizard <u>*is* green</u>.
       L.V.

(*Green* describes the subject *lizard*.)

Grant <u>*was* a Union general in the Civil War</u>.
       L.V.

(*General* identifies the subject *Grant*.)

QUESTION: What are some common linking verbs?

ANSWER: The most frequently used linking verb is *be*, whose forms include the following:

am, are, is, was, were

Of course, verb phrases ending in *be*, *being*, and *been* are also linking verbs, as in these examples:

will be, would be, are being, have been, could have been, etc.

In addition, each of the following verbs can be either an action verb or a linking verb, depending on the way it is used.

VERB	USED AS ACTION VERB	USED AS LINKING VERB
appear	Samuel *appeared* at my door.	He *appeared* upset.
become	That color *becomes* (suits) you.	That color *became* my favorite.
feel	I *felt* sharp rocks underfoot.	I *felt* panicky.
grow	Eliza *grows* vegetables.	Eliza *grows* healthier every day.
look	Snowball looked at the mouse.	The mouse *looked* tasty.
smell	I *smell* a foul odor.	Your feet *smell* bad.
sound	*Sound* the starting bell!	Your comment *sounded* rude.
taste	The chef *tasted* the dough.	The dough *tasted* salty.
turn	I quickly *turned* the page.	The story just *turned* exciting!

Writing Application

Using Linking Verbs

Choose **five** of the verbs in the table above. On a separate sheet of paper, write **two** sentences for each verb. In the first sentence, use the verb as an action verb. In the second sentence, use the verb as a linking verb. Circle each verb, and above it, label it *action* or *linking*.

Samples:

action
a. Do you (smell) a wet dog?

linking
b. The soup (smells) delicious!

QUESTION: How do I identify a linking verb in a sentence?

ANSWER: If a verb can be replaced with some form of the verb *be*, it is a linking verb.

EXAMPLE 1

Is *looks* a linking verb in the following sentence?

The baby *looks* sleepy.   yes

We can replace *looks* with *is* (a form of the verb *be*).

The baby *is* sleepy

Therefore, *looks* in the above sentence is a linking verb.

EXAMPLE 2

Is *looks* a linking verb in the following sentence?

> The jeweler *looks* closely.

In this sentence, we cannot replace *looks* with *is*.

> The jeweler *is* closely

Therefore, *looks* in this sentence is not a linking verb. It is an action verb.

SUMMARY: An *action verb* expresses action, either physical or mental.

A *linking verb* connects the subject with a word in the predicate that describes or identifies the subject.

ACTIVITY 5

Decide whether each underlined verb is an action verb or a linking verb. On the line provided, write A for action verb or L for linking verb.

Samples:

___L___ **a.** As the victor, I <u>felt</u> triumphant.

___A___ **b.** A tornado <u>appeared</u> on the horizon.

___L___ **1.** The sea air <u>smells</u> fresh. *Adj*

___L___ **2.** After the breakup, she <u>looked</u> sad. *Adj.*

___A___ **3.** Suddenly I <u>smelled</u> perfume nearby. *noun*

___A___ **4.** Please <u>turn</u> the hamburgers on the grill. *article*

___L___ **5.** Gradually Hank <u>grew</u> impatient. *Adj.*

ACTIVITY 6

Underline the linking verb in each sentence. Then draw an arrow from the modifying word to the subject that it modifies.

Sample:

At last, everything <u>appears</u> ready.

1. Jess <u>grew</u> tired of Amy's lies.

2. Great! This test <u>looks</u> easy.

3. As usual, the fans <u>are</u> excited.

4. Why do you <u>sound</u> so happy?

5. My sandwich <u>turned</u> soggy by lunchtime.

The box at the right lists 15 action and linking verbs. Using the clues at the bottom of the page, fill in the puzzle. Use each word in the box only once.

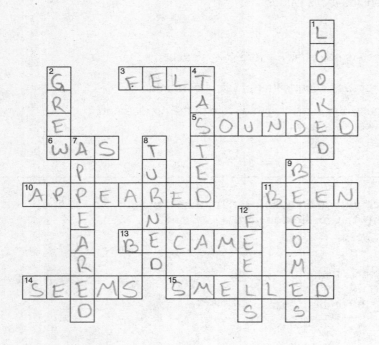

Word box:
- appeared 8
- appeared 8
- became 6
- becomes 7
- been 4
- feels 5
- felt 4
- grew 4
- looked 6
- seems 5
- smelled 7
- sounded 7
- tasted 6
- turned 6
- was 3

ACROSS: Linking Verbs

3. Valentina Tereshkova _____ weightless in space.

5. Paul Revere's warning _____ urgent.

6. Sammy Davis Jr. _____ only five feet, three inches tall.

10. Amelia Earhart _____ hopeful before that final, fateful flight.

11. Golfer Tiger Woods has _____ a sports hero to many.

13. Vincent van Gogh _____ famous for his paintings.

14. Harriet Tubman's life _____ courageous.

15. To the nurse Clara Barton, the filthy battlefield _____ awful.

DOWN: Action Verbs

1. Zebulon Montgomery Pike _____ at the high mountain peak before him.

2. George Washington Carver _____ peanuts.

4. In the 1988 Olympic Games, Jackie Joyner-Kersee _____ victory.

7. To his fans' delight, musician Yo-Yo Ma _____ onstage.

8. Helen Keller _____ her handicaps into a story of success.

9. Albert Einstein's flyaway hair _____ him.

12. Jane Goodall _____ a deep interest in studying chimpanzees.

Helping Verbs and Verb Phrases

Sometimes a verb consists of more than one word.

Shavonne *was writing* a limerick.
     VERB

In the verb *was writing*, *writing* is the **main verb;** *was* is a **helping verb.**

Shavonne *was writing* a limerick.
     H.V.   M.V.

 Helping verbs **come before and "help" the main verb.**

A main verb may have as many as three helping verbs.

ONE HELPING VERB: Shavonne *was* writing a limerick.
                                            H.V.   M.V.

TWO HELPING VERBS: She *has been* writing many limericks.
                                       H.V.   H.V.   M.V.

THREE HELPING VERBS: She *may have been* writing them for you.
                                       H.V.   H.V.   H.V.   M.V.

We have a special name for two or more verbs that work together as one unit: *verb phrase.*

 A *verb phrase* consists of one or more helping verbs plus a main verb.

HELPING VERB(S)	+	MAIN VERB	=	VERB PHRASE
was	+	writing	=	was writing
has been	+	writing	=	has been writing
may have been	+	writing	=	may have been writing

QUESTION: Which verbs can be used as helping verbs?

ANSWER: Below is a list of verbs commonly used as helping verbs (also called *auxiliary verbs*). Note that forms of *be*, which we studied earlier as linking verbs, can also function as helping verbs.

Commonly Used Helping Verbs

FORMS OF BE: am, is, are, was, were, be, being, been

FORMS OF HAVE: have, has, had

FORMS OF DO: do, does, did

MODALS: will, would, shall, should, may, might, must, can, could

The last category of helping verbs in the list above is modals. The modals help a main verb express an attitude (such as doubt, certainty, obligation) toward the action or state of being.

MODALS: Kahlil *should* sing the solo.

(The modal *should* helps the main verb, *sing,* indicate that Kahlil *ought* to do something.)

On the math test, students *must* show their calculations.

(The modal *must* helps the main verb, *show,* indicate that students *are required to* do something.)

In this book, you are not required to identify a verb as a modal. Instead, your goal is to identify helping verbs, main verbs, and verb phrases, and to practice using them.

ACTIVITY 8 _____

Underline the verb phrase in each sentence. Then, on the lines provided, write the helping verb(s) and the main verb.

Sample:		
	HELPING	MAIN
Your coat <u>may have been stolen</u>.	*may have been*	*stolen*

	HELPING	MAIN
1. The price of a movie ticket has gone up.	_____	_____
2. Last night, a hyena was laughing.	_____	_____
3. Greta can be trusted with a secret.	_____	_____
4. Soon, you will blow the whistle.	_____	_____
5. Nobody would have believed me.	_____	_____
6. This meat should have been cooked longer.	_____	_____
7. I shall try my best!	_____	_____
8. At daybreak, the ranger will be hiking the trail.	_____	_____
9. This car must have been hit with hail.	_____	_____
10. Yes, I did paint the dog's toenails.	_____	_____

When you completed Activity 8, did you notice that the main verb is always the last word in the verb phrase? You will find that this observation always holds true, even in a sentence that asks a question.

Word Order in Questions

In questions, we usually put the subject after the first helping verb.

<u>*Did*</u> <u>*you*</u> <u>*paint*</u> the dog's toenails?
H.V. S.   M.V.

(The subject *you* comes after the helping verb *Did*. The main verb *paint* comes after the subject.)

<u>Have</u> *you* <u>been painting</u> the dog's toenails?
   H.V.   S.   H.V.   M.V.

(The subject *you* comes after the first helping verb, *Have*. The second helping verb, *been*, and the main verb, *painting*, come after the subject.)

ACTIVITY 9

Underline the verb phrase in each sentence. Then, circle the main verb.

> **Samples:**
>
> **a.** <u>Has</u> the new music store <u>been (getting)</u> much business?
>
> **b.** <u>Does</u> the five o'clock train (stop) at Orange Station?

1. Will somebody lend me a pencil?

2. Should Paul get a job?

3. Has Dr. Sands explained the test results?

4. Can that straw basket hold a dozen eggs?

5. Have you been drinking out of the milk jug?

6. Do the geese in that pond fly south for the winter?

7. Had Betsy been sneaking off campus during lunch?

8. Did the new math teacher learn everyone's name?

9. Should students have been invited to the meeting?

10. Would you have been offended by her comment?

ACTIVITY 10

Change each statement to a question.

> **Sample:**
>
> The team captain has been named.
>
> <u>Has the team captain been named?</u>

1. The school nurse will call your mom.

_____

2. We can stay out until ten o'clock.

_____

3. Alexandra has been saving for her first car.

_____

4. This study guide does have an answer key.

_____

5. The plumber should have arrived by now.

_____

Reminder: Did you end each of your questions in Activity 10 with a question mark?

Writing
Application

Using Verb Phrases in Questions

With your teacher's approval, pair up with someone in class. On a sheet of paper, write **five** questions you would like your classmate to answer. Examples are _Are you going to the dance Friday night?_ and _Did you do the math homework?_ Underline the verb phrase in each question.

   Then exchange papers with each other. Using complete sentences, write answers to each of the questions you receive. Underline the verb or verb phrase in each sentence. Finally, share the results with your classmate.

Composition Hint

In your writing, aim for _conciseness_—brief, uncluttered expression. For example, you can often shorten a verb phrase when its meaning is clear in context (in the surrounding sentences). By doing so, you avoid _wordiness_—the use of unnecessary words.

WORDY: Janet refused to share. She _should have shared._

CONCISE: Janet refused to share. She _should have._

             (The main verb _shared_ is understood.)

WORDY: If José does not confess, I _will confess._

CONCISE: If José does not confess, I _will._

             (The main verb _confess_ is understood.)

   Besides shortening the verb phrase, you can sometimes omit (leave out) an object that follows it. (You will learn more about objects in Lesson 6.) In the following example, notice that _it_ is omitted from the revised sentence.

WORDY: The young people understood the joke, but the adults _did_ not _understand_ it.

CONCISE: The young people understood the joke, but the adults _did_ not.

             (The main verb _understand_ is understood, and the object _it_ is understood.)

Make each sentence more concise by shortening a verb phrase.

> **Sample:**
>
> Heather could have lied about it, but she did not lie.
>
> <u>Heather could have lied about it, but she did not.</u>

1. If you do not ask, I will ask.

_____

2. Freddie would not admit it, but he should have admitted it.

_____

3. Lola could have helped, and she should have helped.

_____

4. Ms. Valdez should have been thanked; she was not thanked.

_____

5. If Zelda didn't tell you, then who did tell you?

_____

Verbs in Contractions

Suppose a teacher asks you who broke the classroom window. You did not see who did it. What would you say to the teacher?

1. I do not know.

2. I don't know.

You would probably use the words in choice 2, *I don't know*. In this sentence, *don't* is a contraction.

 A *contraction* is a combination of two words with one or more letters omitted.

In informal conversation, we tend to use contractions. For example, we combine *do* with *not,* forming the contraction *don't*. Note that *not,* the second word in the contraction, loses the letter *o,* and in place of that *o* we use an apostrophe: **don't.**

Many contractions consist of a verb plus *not*. The word *not* is never part of the verb in a sentence. *Not* is an adverb that modifies the verb. (You will learn more about adverbs in Lesson 10.) Therefore, when you identify the verb in a sentence, do not include *not*.

Hillary *does* not *believe* your campaign promises. (The verb is *does believe*.)

We *were*n't there during the rally. (The verb is *were*.)

Maxine *did*n't *vote* for Erik. (The verb is *did vote*.)

*Has*n't Kareem *cast* his vote yet? (The verb is *Has cast*.)

On the line provided, write the verb in each sentence.

> **Samples:**
>
> **a.** Ronny and Gwen don't play sports. _do play_
>
> **b.** Didn't Aaron hit a home run? _Did hit_

1. Andrew couldn't hit the basket. _____

2. Vikki wasn't nervous before the game. _____

3. Won't you watch the volleyball game? _____

4. Don't swing at the ball so soon. _____

5. Kristin hadn't seen the new uniforms yet. _____

6. They weren't listening to Coach Warren. _____

7. Shouldn't somebody keep score? _____

8. Hank isn't playing the quarterback position. _____

9. My tennis balls aren't in my gym bag. _____

10. Wasn't that soccer game fabulous? _____

Of course, verbs may form contractions with words besides _not_.

You'_ll hear_ from me on Tuesday.

(The verb is _will hear_. The subject is _You_.)

By lunchtime, they_'d walked_ five miles.

(The verb is _had walked_. The subject is _they_.)

The following verbs can be contracted, as shown, with words besides _not_:

Verb	Contracted Form	Example
have	've	they've
has	's	he's
had	'd	we'd
am	'm	I'm
is	's	he's
are	're	you're
will	'll	she'll

Contractions

In the table on page 30, notice that *has* and *is* are both contracted as *'s*. In a sentence, the difference in meaning becomes clear through context, or other words.

1. *She's* a thoughtful person. (Since *She has a thoughtful person* makes no sense, we know that *She's* means *She is*.)

2. *She's* been thoughtful to me. (Since *She is been thoughtful* makes little sense, we know that *She's* means *She has*.)

In standard English, we do not combine *was* or *were* with any word besides *not*. Doing so would create the same contraction as adding *is* or *are*, and confusion could result. Instead, we write or speak the words separately.

3. *He was* late. (NOT *He's,* which means *he is*)

4. *They were* early. (NOT *They're,* which means *they are*)

If you become confused about how to form a contraction, or whether to form one, remember this: It is always acceptable to spell out (or say) the words separately. You do not have to use the contraction. When in doubt, spell it out.

ACTIVITY 13

On the line provided, write the verb in each sentence.

Samples:

a. He'd always been fearful of snakes. _had been_

b. It's ruining my entire day! _is ruining_

1. After the race, they'll need water. _____

2. She'd known him for ten years. _____

3. Right now, he's solving algebra problems. _____

4. We've suspected you of sneakiness. _____

5. Fortunately, this'll soon be over. _____

6. Yes, she's helping me with the decorations. _____

7. In my opinion, they've done a great job. _____

8. We're meeting for dinner and a movie. _____

9. Well, I'm not certain of the correct answer. _____

10. As always, they're sitting in the back row. _____

4 Compound Verbs

 A *compound verb* consists of two or more verbs of the same subject connected by *and, or,* or *but.*

The <u>artist</u> <u>sketched *and* painted</u>.
    s.   COMPOUND VERB

The verb *sketched* tells what the subject *artist* did.

The verb *painted* tells what else the subject *artist* did.

These two verbs of the same subject, connected by *and,* are the compound verb *sketched and painted.*

Here are more examples of compound verbs.

<u>Nicholas</u> <u>wrote, revised, *and* polished</u> the essay.
   s.   COMPOUND VERB

Each morning, the <u>athlete</u> <u>runs *or* swims</u> laps.
         s.   COMPOUND VERB

The <u>radio</u> <u>works *but* has</u> a lot of static.
     s. COMPOUND VERB

ACTIVITY 1

Underline the compound verb in each sentence. Then circle the connecting word.

Sample:

    All spring, weeds <u>sprouted, grew, (and) thrived</u> in my yard.

1. Ella <u>found (and) trapped</u> the rat.

2. Desperately, he <u>begged, borrowed, (or) stole</u> the necessary money.

3. All night, <u>thunder boomed (and) rumbled</u> overhead.

4. On the street, Ms. Garret <u>smiled (but) walked</u> on by me.

5. Francine, either <u>eat (or) leave</u> the table.

Often, the parts of a compound verb are separated by other words in the predicate. Do not be distracted by these other words when you identify the compound verb.

I <u>studied</u> the Civil War *and <u>wrote</u>* a report on it.

(The compound verb is *studied and wrote.*)

Each weekend I <u>went</u> to the library *or* <u>surfed</u> the Internet.

(The compound verb is *went or surfed.*)

Write the compound verb of each sentence on the line provided. Include the connecting word.

> **Sample:**
>
> Susie King Taylor was fourteen years old and lived in Georgia.
>
> _____ *was and lived* _____

1. Susie was a slave but soon gained freedom.

   _____ was and gained _____

2. In July 1863, Susie met Clara Barton and assisted this nurse.

   _____ met and assisted _____

3. Union soldiers marched to Georgia, attacked Fort Pulaski, and freed Susie's family.

   _____ marched, attacked and freed _____

4. Many former slaves joined the Union Army or aided the soldiers.

   _____ joined and aided _____

5. Young Susie fed soldiers, cleaned wounds, and washed uniforms.

   _____ fed, cleaned and washed _____

Compound verbs may include verb phrases.   *Antonio Contreras*

   Grandpa *will shop* for gifts or *bake* the fruitcake.

Samanta Wilchey is in elgin right now

(The compound verb is *will shop or bake*.)

Compound verbs may be separated by other words in a question or when the adverb *not* is used.

   Will Grandpa *shop* for gifts or *bake* the fruitcake?

(The compound verb is *Will shop or bake*.)

   Grandpa *won't shop* for gifts or *bake* the fruitcake.

(To find the verb, separate the contraction into the words *will not*. The adverb *not* is not part of the verb. The compound verb is *will shop or bake*.)

The understood subject *you* can have a compound verb.

   Give me liberty or *give* me death!

(The compound verb is *Give or give*.)

When there are more than two verbs in a compound verb, place a comma after each one except the last.

   The traveler *has bought* a ticket, *boarded* the train, and *found* a seat.

(The compound verb is *has bought, boarded, and found*.)

In each sentence, underline each verb in the compound verb.

> **Samples:**
>
> **a.** <u>Weren't</u> you <u>buying</u> lumber and <u>building</u> a bookcase today?
>
> **b.** Please <u>watch</u> the children but <u>don't</u> <u>feed</u> them sweets.

1. In the ice rink, the skater has been leaping and twirling.

2. Fortunately, no one was hurt or injured in the accident.

3. This eggplant should be washed, sliced, and baked with cheese.

4. Help me trim the hedge, or go somewhere else.

5. Didn't Rudy call Leon and talk about basketball tryouts?

6. The tomatoes should have tasted delicious but tasted overripe instead.

7. You may collect food donations, record the donations, or box them up.

8. The sedan should have been washed and waxed yesterday.

9. Have your teachers called or spoken with your parents this year?

10. Bring me the can of pink paint but don't step in that spill.

 Writing
Application

Using Compound Verbs

On a sheet of paper, make a list of **ten** verbs. Group them in related pairs, such as *snore, sleep* or *smile, wave.* With your teacher's approval, exchange papers with a classmate. Using the verbs your classmate listed, write **five** sentences that each have a compound verb. Share the results with your classmate.

Composition Hint

A common error in writing is unnecessary repetition of the subject.

Kim sat down. *Kim* tuned the guitar. *Kim* selected sheet music. (three *Kims*)

With a compound verb, we can avoid such repetition.

Kim sat down, tuned the guitar, and selected sheet music. (one *Kim*)

Combine each group of sentences into one sentence. Use a compound verb to eliminate repetition of the subject.

Samples:

a. Didn't Madelyn clean her room?

Didn't Madelyn sweep the floor?

Didn't Madelyn clean her room or sweep the floor?

b. Sparky can sit.

Sparky can shake hands.

Sparky can fetch.

Sparky can sit, shake hands, and fetch.

1. I love expensive clothes.

I can't afford them.

I love expensive clothes but I can't afford them.

2. My brother can repair clocks.

My brother can install a doorbell.

My brother can repair clocks and install a doorbell.

3. Have you ever spotted a UFO?

Have you ever seen an alien?

Have you ever spotted a UFO or seen an alien?

4. The elephant is filling her trunk with water.

The elephant is spraying her back.

The elephant is filling her trunk with water and spraying her back.

5. Frida loves jazz.

Frida tolerates rap.

Frida hates country and western.

Frida loves jazz, tolerates rap but hates country and western.

6. The Colorado River has risen.

The Colorado River has overflowed its banks.

The Colorado River has risen and overflowed its banks.

7. A swarm of ants found the dead bug.

A swarm of ants picked it apart.

A swarm of ants stored the food.

A swarm of ants found the dead bug and picked it apart.

8. Can't you tutor me in math?

Can't you give me some tips?

Can't you tutor me in math and give some tips?

9. Do parakeets sing all day?

Do parakeets rest all day?

Do parakeets sing all day or rest all day?

10. Tony will crack open the coconut.   _____

Tony will drain the milk.   _____

Tony will pry out the meat.

QUESTION: May a sentence have both a compound subject and a compound verb?

ANSWER: Yes. Here is an example:

Patricia *and* Max wrote *and* illustrated a storybook.
COMPOUND SUBJECT   COMPOUND VERB

Do foxes *or* coyotes sometimes hunt *and* eat rabbits?
C.V. COMPOUND SUBJECT   COMPOUND VERB

ACTIVITY 5

In each sentence, underline the subject once and underline the verb twice. Be sure to watch for compound subjects and predicates. The first sentence is completed for you as a sample.

Today in America, women can vote, own property, and go to college. However, these rights have not always been a fact of life. In the early 1800s, girls and women received little education. Colleges and universities normally would not admit them. Certainly, no female of any age could vote. Land, houses, and other property were normally held in men's names. Fathers, husbands, and brothers controlled these possessions for "their women."

Some women and men didn't agree with this state of affairs. Two women in particular fought for women's rights. In 1848, Elizabeth Cady Stanton and Lucretia Mott planned and organized the first women's rights convention. It was held in Seneca Falls, New York, in July 1848.

At the meeting, supporters and critics of women's rights came together. Energetically, they discussed social, civil, and religious rights of women. The discussions and debates inspired similar meetings across the country. For fifty years, Stanton led the campaign for women's rights in America. She died in 1902. In 1920, women finally were granted suffrage (the right to vote).

Using Compound Subjects
and Compound Verbs

What is one right or privilege you *wish* you had, but don't have? Perhaps this right is denied you by family rules, school rules, city laws, or another authority.

On a separate sheet of paper, write a paragraph of at least **seven** sentences, explaining the right you wish you had, why it is denied you, and what, if anything, you could do to change matters. Use at least one compound subject and one compound verb. In each sentence, underline the subject <u>once</u> and the verb <u>twice</u>.

5 Nouns

The purpose of nouns is to identify or name things.

 A *noun* is a word that names a person, place, thing, animal, or idea.

PERSONS: girl, Tabitha, doctor, baby

PLACES: lake, New York City, home, America

THINGS: desk, zipper, apple, e-mail

ANIMALS: tiger, Buster, snake, catfish

IDEAS: happiness, fear, exhaustion, responsibility

Sentences may contain one or more nouns. How many nouns can you identify in the following sentence?

In the huge theater, a dancer wearing red shoes stepped onto the stage with confidence.

The sentence uses a variety of nouns: *theater* (place), *dancer* (person), *shoes* (things), *stage* (place), and *confidence* (idea).

ACTIVITY 1

This organizer shows the different kinds of nouns. In each petal of the flower, write <u>three</u> examples of the stated kind of noun. For example, in the *idea* petal you might write *honesty, confusion,* and *fame*. Try to write nouns that are not already used in this lesson!

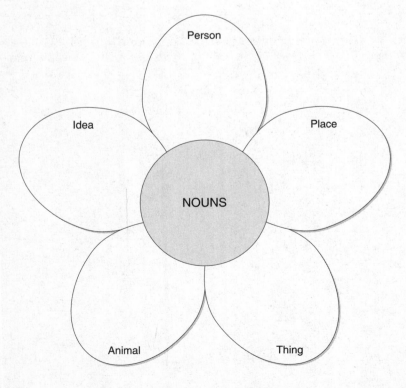

ACTIVITY 2

Refer to the nouns you listed in Activity 1. On the lines below, write five sentences. In each sentence, use one or more nouns from Activity 1. (You can use additional nouns, too.) Circle each noun in your sentences.

> **Sample:**
>
> Our (departure) was marked by (hugs) and (kisses) from both (parents.)

1. _____

2. _____

3. _____

4. _____

5. _____

Some nouns name things that we can see, touch, and hear, such as *sky, door,* and *music.* These nouns are called **concrete nouns**. Other nouns name things we cannot see or touch, such as *luck, temperament,* and *idea.* These nouns are called **abstract nouns**. Here are a few more examples of concrete and abstract nouns:

CONCRETE: stairs, smoke, sound, whisper, stomach

ABSTRACT: hope, certainty, vision, temperament, intention

For many people, identifying abstract nouns is a challenge. It may help to realize that many abstract nouns name a state of being or feeling, such as *hope, certainty,* and *intention* above and others such as *anger, passion, thirst,* and *hunger.*

ACTIVITY 3

Underline each noun in the following passage, which continues on page 40 (there are 25 nouns in all). Then, write each noun in the appropriate column—Concrete or Abstract. One noun is done for you.

Hint: The title and each name count as one noun each.

	CONCRETE NOUNS	ABSTRACT NOUNS
Help Me, Helen! by Helen DeRosa **Dear Helen:** Help! My (so-called) best friend is stealing my boyfriend. How could these people betray me in such a dastardly <u>fashion</u>? Should I offer forgiveness, or serve up a little revenge? Or should I just quietly dump my pal *and* my sweetheart? Signed, Bitten by Betrayal in Atlanta		*fashion*

CONCRETE NOUNS	ABSTRACT NOUNS

Dear Bitten: Bite back! My suggestion: Send a note to each betrayer. Tell each person you want to talk privately, but name the same place and time in each message. Then, hide nearby and watch. Upon their <u>arrival</u>, enjoy their looks of dismay when they realize you've seen into their wicked hearts!

Helen

arrival

QUESTION: May a noun consist of more than one word?

ANSWER: Yes. Nouns of more than one word are called **compound nouns**. A compound noun may be written as one word, as separate words, or as a hyphenated word. However it is written, a compound noun names one thing.

ONE WORD: cornflakes, notebook, spoonful, breakthrough

SEPARATE WORDS: Los Angeles, post office, lily pad, dining room

HYPHENATED WORDS: great-grandpa, self-esteem, yo-yo, light-year

ACTIVITY 4

In each sentence, underline each noun. Then write the compound noun on the line provided.

Sample:

My <u>preference</u> is <u>books</u> about <u>teens</u>, such as *A Separate Peace*.

compound noun: ___*A Separate Peace*___

1. Mick, please get the vacuum cleaner out of the closet.

   compound noun: _____

2. His sister-in-law works as a nurse in a clinic.

   compound noun: _____

3. A slithery snake slyly escaped from the zoo around lunchtime.

   compound noun: _____

4. All departures from the airport are delayed due to bad weather.

   compound noun: _____

5. In their sandwiches, would your friends like peanut butter or turkey?

   compound noun: _____

Some words may be used as either a noun or a verb.

NOUN: Two *cooks* prepared a delicious meal.

VERB: Mike *cooks* fabulous Chinese pot stickers.

NOUN: The soy sauce is there by your right *hand*.

VERB: *Hand* me a pair of chopsticks.

ACTIVITY 5 _____

Look at the underlined word. If it is used as a noun, write N on the line provided. If it is used as a verb, write V.

Samples:

a. Can we <u>fish</u> off this pier? _____V_____

b. The lake is swimming with <u>fish</u>! _____N_____

1. a. There is a <u>crack</u> in the window. _____

  b. <u>Crack</u> these eggs into the pan. _____

2. a. A <u>fly</u> landed on my salad. _____

  b. Next week we <u>fly</u> to Oregon. _____

3. a. Please <u>paste</u> photos in the album. _____

  b. <u>Paste</u> is thicker than glue. _____

4. a. She <u>tests</u> the smoke detector monthly. _____

  b. How did you do on the midterm <u>tests</u>? _____

5. a. Millie has a lovely <u>smile</u>. _____

  b. The twins <u>smile</u> at everyone. _____

Common and Proper Nouns

Nouns may be either common or proper. Compare the following sentences.

1. On which street do I turn?

2. Turn on Beach Street.

In Sentence 1, *street* is a **common noun**. In Sentence 2, *Beach Street* is a **proper noun**.

 A *proper noun* names *one particular* person, place, thing, or animal.

A proper noun is *always* capitalized.

In the example above, *Beach Street* is a proper noun. It refers to one particular street. Notice that both words in the proper noun are capitalized.

A *common noun* refers to no particular person, place, thing, animal, or idea.

A common noun is *not* capitalized.

In the previous example, *street* is a common noun. Notice that it is not capitalized. The common noun *street* can refer to any street. It does not refer to a particular street.

Here are some examples of common nouns and proper nouns.

COMMON NOUNS	PROPER NOUNS
(*not* capitalized)	(*always* capitalized)
man	Paul Bunyan
month	April
canyon	Grand Canyon
monument	Statue of Liberty
girl	Anne Frank
horse	Black Beauty
school	Washington High School
ocean	Atlantic Ocean
book	*Treasure Island*
nation	United States of America

ACTIVITY 6

Complete the table by writing common nouns and proper nouns on the appropriate blanks.

COMMON NOUNS	PROPER NOUNS
Samples:	
a. country	<u>Argentina</u>
b. <u>era</u>	Victorian Era
1. city	_____
2. _____	Mary
3. day	_____
4. president	_____
5. _____	Jupiter
6. _____	Olympic Games
7. language	_____

8. _____ Mississippi River

9. magazine _____

10. state _____

ACTIVITY 7 _____

In the following passage, underline each noun. For proper nouns, add correct capitalization by crossing out lowercase letters and writing capital letters above them. The first sentence is completed for you as a sample.

           G   L   N   A   U

The <u>great lakes</u> of <u>north america</u> sit like a <u>crown</u> over the northern <u>border</u> of the <u>united</u>

S

<u>states</u>. Four of the lakes (all but lake michigan) sprawl across the boundary between the

united states and canada.

    Of the five lakes, lake erie is shallowest, reaching a maximum depth of only 210 feet.

The lake's shallowness and its famous storminess have brought many ships to ruin. In fact,

the lake has been called the marine graveyard of the inland seas. Despite its dangerous

waters, the lake has four major ports. These are located at detroit, michigan; buffalo, new

york; cleveland, ohio; and toledo, ohio. In buffalo, lake erie dumps over niagara falls into

lake ontario, the smallest of the great lakes.

✏️ Writing Application

Using Common and Proper Nouns

Complete the following job application. Each time you write a proper noun, circle it.

Application for Employment
Sno-Cones on Wheels
We Bring the Fun to You!

Personal Information

Name: (first) _____ (middle) _____ (last) _____

Street Address: _____

City: _____ State: _____ Zip: _____

Home Phone: (_____) _____

Have you ever applied for employment with us?

Yes: _____ No: _____ If yes, when? _____

Position Desired

(check one) _____ Sno-Cone Maker _____ Party Coordinator _____ Accountant _____ Manager

Desired Salary: $_____

If you prefer to work in a different zip code than where you currently live, please indicate below where you would like to be located.

City: _____ State: _____ Zip: _____

Work Eligibility

Are you eligible to work in the United States? Yes: _____ No: _____

Are you available to work holidays? Yes: _____ No: _____

When will you be available to begin work? _____/_____ (Month/Year)

Are you 16 or older? Yes: _____ No: _____

Do you have special training or skills (additional spoken or written languages, computer software knowledge, machine operation experience, etc.)?

_____

_____

How did you hear of our organization?

_____

Availability

List the days you are available to work: _____

_____

Total Weekly Hours Available: _____ Hours Available: from _____ to _____

Education

High School: _____ City: _____ State: _____

College: _____ City: _____ State: _____

Course of Study: _____ # of Years Completed: _____

Did you graduate? Yes: _____ No: _____ Degree: _____

To answer each of the following questions, refer to the employment application you completed in the Writing Application on pages 43–44. For items 1, 4, and 5, write your answer in complete sentences.

1. Why do you think the employment application requires so many proper nouns to be filled in?

   _____

   _____

2. Do the proper nouns begin with capital letters or lowercase letters? _____

3. List three examples of common nouns that are capitalized on the application form.

   _____   _____   _____

4. Why do you think the form uses capital letters for some common nouns?

   _____

   _____

5. What is the best way to tell whether a noun is common or proper?

   _____

   _____

6 Nouns as Direct and Indirect Objects

In Lesson 1, we examined nouns used as subjects in sentences. In this lesson, we examine nouns used as direct objects and indirect objects.

Nouns as Direct Objects

How is the noun *football* used in these two sentences?

1. The *football* fell from the shelf.

2. Nigel kicked the *football*.

In sentence 1, the noun *football* is the **subject** of the verb *fell*. In sentence 2, the noun *football* is the **direct object** of the verb *kicked*.

 A *direct object* **is a word in the predicate that receives the action of the verb.**

In sentence 2 above, the noun *football* is the word in the predicate that receives the action of the verb *kicked*. Therefore, the noun *football* is the direct object of the verb *kicked*. Here are more examples of direct objects in sentences.

Megan kissed *Justin*. (*Justin* is the direct object of the verb *kissed*.)

A bee gathered *pollen*. (*Pollen* is the direct object of the verb *gathered*.)

My dog loves *cheese*. (*Cheese* is the direct object of the verb *loves*.)

As you can see, the type of action the direct object receives may be physical (*kissed, gathered*) or mental (*loves*). Direct objects always follow action verbs, never linking verbs. Compare the noun *eggs* in these two sentences.

Her breakfast was *eggs*.

Joann burned the *eggs*.

The first sentence cannot have a direct object because it has no action verb; *was* does not express any action. Therefore, *eggs* in this sentence is not a direct object.

On the other hand, the second sentence can have a direct object because it has an action verb; *burned* expresses action. In this sentence, *eggs* receives the action of the verb *burned* and is a direct object of that verb.

Joann burned the *eggs*.
S.   V.   D.O.

QUESTION: Are there other verbs, besides *was,* that do not express action?

ANSWER: Yes. Remember that linking verbs do not express action, as you learned in Lesson 3. *Was* is a linking verb, and so are the other forms of the verb *be*, as listed here:

am, is, are, was, were, be, being, been

Certain verb phrases that include being verbs are used as linking, not action, verbs. Study these linking verb phrases:

will be	should be	can be	has been
shall be	may be	could be	had been
would be	might be	have been	will have been

Remember this about *be* verbs:
- *Be* verbs do not express action.
- *Be* verbs cannot have a direct object.

Only action verbs can have direct objects. However, not every action verb in every sentence has a direct object. It all depends on how the verb is used.

Joann *burned* the eggs.

(The action verb *burned* has a direct object, *eggs*.)

The fire *burned* brightly.

(The action verb *burned* does not have a direct object. The word *brightly* is not a noun; it is an adverb that describes the verb.)

How Can I Find Direct Objects?

To find the direct object, ask the question WHAT? or WHOM? right after the action verb.

EXAMPLE 1

What is the direct object in the following sentence?

Carlton types his essays on a computer.

QUESTION:	Carlton types WHAT?
ANSWER:	Carlton types essays.
DIRECT OBJECT:	*essays*

EXAMPLE 2

What is the direct object in the following sentence?

Cold rain drove the swimmers indoors.

QUESTION:	Rain drove WHOM?
ANSWER:	Rain drove the swimmers.
DIRECT OBJECT:	*swimmers*

ACTIVITY 1 _____

Underline the verb in each sentence. Then draw an arrow from the verb to the direct object. The first three sentences have hints to help you.

Sample:

Rory <u>pushed</u> a red wheelbarrow up the hill.

1. Each day, Granddad winds his old clock. *(Granddad winds WHAT?)*

2. At their meeting, Jean praised her employees. *(Jean praised WHOM?)*

3. Buster was wagging his tail happily. *(Buster was wagging WHAT?)*

4. Quickly Hector chose Clint for his team.

5. Suddenly the volcano spewed lava.

6. I marked my place in the book.

7. Overnight, a snow drift covered the old cabin.

8. A new signal light will direct traffic at the corner.

9. Salty waves caressed the sandy beach.

10. Effortlessly, the magician amazed her audience.

ACTIVITY 2

In which sentence, *a* or *b*, is the underlined noun a direct object? Write D.O. on the proper line.

> **Samples:**
>
> _____ **a.** What will be the <u>name</u> of the new athletic field?
>
> _D. O._ **b.** Unfortunately, I forgot your <u>name</u>.

1. _____ **a.** Jack and Jill carried <u>water</u> in pails.

   _____ **b.** At meals, your only beverage should be <u>water</u>.

2. _____ **a.** Rene's native language is <u>French</u>, of course.

   _____ **b.** Paulo studied <u>French</u> all afternoon.

3. _____ **a.** Your words are just empty <u>promises</u>.

   _____ **b.** I believed your <u>promises</u> until recently.

4. _____ **a.** With irritation, Latifah slapped <u>mosquitoes</u> on her arms.

   _____ **b.** Those pesky insects were <u>mosquitoes</u>, right?

5. _____ **a.** These antique cloths may have been <u>napkins</u>.

   _____ **b.** Please fold the <u>napkins</u> into fancy shapes.

A direct object may be **compound**—that is, it may consist of more than one word. Use the WHAT? and WHOM? question to find a compound direct object, just as you would with a single direct object.

EXAMPLE 3

What is the direct object in the following sentence?

Carlton types his essays and letters on a computer.

QUESTION: Carlton types WHAT?

ANSWER: Carlton types essays and letters.

DIRECT OBJECT: *essays and letters*

EXAMPLE 4

What is the direct object in the following sentence?

Cold rain drove the swimmers and sunbathers indoors.

QUESTION: Rain drove WHOM?

ANSWER: Rain drove the swimmers and sunbathers.

DIRECT OBJECT: *swimmers and sunbathers*

ACTIVITY 3

In each sentence, underline the verb. Then write the direct object on the line provided. Some sentences have a compound direct object. The first three sentences give you a hint in parentheses.

Samples:

	DIRECT OBJECT
a. Jackie Robinson <u>broke</u> the race barrier in baseball.	*race barrier*
b. He <u>inspired</u> fans and teammates with his courage.	*fans and teammates*

1. A "color barrier" once blocked African Americans from major-league baseball teams. (The color barrier blocked WHOM?) _____

2. In the 1940s, major-league baseball allowed only white players. (Major-league baseball allowed WHOM?) _____

3. However, Branch Rickey rejected this unfair rule and foolish attitude. (Rickey rejected WHAT?) _____

4. Rickey held the position of team president of the Brooklyn Dodgers. _____

5. He signed Jackie Robinson to the Montreal Royals, a farm team. _____

6. In 1947, Robinson received a new uniform and new teammates. _____

7. He played his first major-league game for the Brooklyn Dodgers. _____

8. The brave athlete faced some angry baseball fans and teammates.

_____

9. His presence on the field pleased other people.

_____

10. By the end the season, he had earned the Rookie of the Year award and new respect.

_____

Writing Application

Using Direct Objects

Have you ever done something that was unpopular, but you knew you were right to do it? On a separate sheet of paper, write a paragraph of at least **five** sentences explaining what you did, why it was unpopular, and why you did it anyway. Use at least **three** direct objects and underline each one.

Nouns as Indirect Objects

How is the noun *Fred* used in the following sentence?

Aunt Jennifer made *Fred* some pancakes.
    S.   V.   ?   D.O.

Fred is the **indirect object** of the verb *made*.

 An *indirect object* is a word in the predicate that tells FOR WHOM OR WHAT or TO WHOM OR WHAT something was done, is being done, or will be done.

In the example above, note that two nouns follow the action verb *made: Fred* and *pancakes.* The noun *pancakes* is the **direct object** of *made* because it answers the question WHAT? (Aunt Jennifer made WHAT? She made *pancakes.*)

The noun *Fred* is the **indirect object** of the verb *made. Fred* tells FOR WHOM Aunt Jennifer made pancakes. (Aunt Jennifer made pancakes FOR WHOM? For *Fred.*)

Aunt Jennifer made *Fred* some pancakes.
    S.   V.   I.O.   D.O.

The sentence about pancakes and Fred shows this important fact:

• An action verb can have both a *direct object* and an *indirect object* in the same sentence.

Here are more examples of indirect objects in sentences.

The bluebird gave its *baby* a worm.
                      I.O.   D.O.

George told *Anna* a lie.
              I.O.   D.O.

Should I send the *mayor* a letter?
                    I.O.   D.O.

In each sentence, the verb is underlined and the direct object is italicized. Circle the indirect object.

> **Sample:**
>
> Mr. Harper <u>paid</u> the (babysitter) a *bonus*.

1. That embarrassing mistake <u>taught</u> Kirsten a *lesson*.

2. Thoughtfully, Derek <u>saved</u> Royce a *seat*.

3. Those mountains <u>bring</u> the region many *tourists*.

4. <u>Send</u> Coach Rawlings the *bill*, please.

5. The sun <u>gave</u> the lake a golden *glow*.

How Can I Find the Indirect Object?

To find the indirect object, ask the question TO WHOM OR WHAT? or FOR WHOM OR WHAT?

EXAMPLE 1

What is the indirect object in the following sentence?

> The team promised the fans a victory.
>
> QUESTION: The team promised a victory TO WHOM?
>
> ANSWER: to the fans
>
> INDIRECT OBJECT: *fans*

EXAMPLE 2

What is the indirect object in the following sentence?

> We bought the motorcycle a seat.
>
> QUESTION: We bought a seat FOR WHAT?
>
> ANSWER: for the motorcycle
>
> INDIRECT OBJECT: *motorcycle*

QUESTION: Can an indirect object be compound?

ANSWER: Yes, an indirect object can consist of two or more nouns.

> The crowd gave the *actor and director* applause.
>   COMPOUND I.O.   D.O.

EXAMPLE 3

What is the indirect object in the following sentence?

The team promised the coach and fans a victory.

QUESTION: The team promised a victory TO WHOM?

ANSWER: to the coach and fans

INDIRECT OBJECT: *coach and fans*

ACTIVITY 5 _____

Underline the verb in each sentence. Then write the indirect object on the I.O. line, and write the direct object on the D.O. line. Remember, objects may be compound. Some sentences do not have an indirect object.

Samples:

a. Dan <u>handed</u> Helen and Stacy some soap and rags. I.O. *Helen and Stacy*

D.O. *soap and rags*

b. Please <u>make</u> a lesson plan for the substitute. I.O. *none*

D.O. *lesson plan*

1. James built Monica a dollhouse. I.O. _____

D.O. _____

2. The storyteller told the group a tall tale. I.O. _____

D.O. _____

3. Please give the dog and the puppy a bath. I.O. _____

D.O. _____

4. A stone sent ripples across the water. I.O. _____

D.O. _____

5. The caterer offered the host and guests dessert. I.O. _____

D.O. _____

6. Barbara carved fish and birds out of soap. I.O _____

D.O. _____

7. He awarded Eric and Sonya first place and second place. I.O. _____

D.O. _____

8. We provided our guests a fantastic party.

I.O. _____

D.O. _____

9. Did gophers destroy the garden again?

I.O. _____

D.O. _____

10. Tall trees provided the campers shelter.

I.O. _____

D.O. _____

QUESTION: Which comes first in a sentence, the direct object or the indirect object?

ANSWER: The indirect object *always* comes before the direct object.

This sentence expresses a thought without using an indirect object:

Mr. Kincaid teaches karate to my cousin.
D.O.

(This sentence has a direct object, *karate,* but no indirect object.)

We can rewrite the sentence to express the same thought using an indirect object. Notice where the indirect object is placed in the sentence.

Mr. Kincaid teaches my *cousin* karate.
I.O.   D.O.

(The indirect object *cousin* comes before the direct object *karate.*)

ACTIVITY 6

Rewrite each sentence, changing the italicized expression to an indirect object.

> **Sample:**
>
> Did the principal offer a choice *to the students*?
>
> _Did the principal offer the students a choice?_

1. Nadine offered a ride *to Missy*.

_____

2. I saved a seat *for my friend*.

_____

3. Wildflowers give beauty *to the field*.

_____

4. The wolf found a safe den *for her pups*.

_____

5. Have you sent a thank-you note *to Grandma*?

_____

6. Please write some instructions *for the travelers*.

_____

7. Heavy clouds brought rain *to the thirsty fields*.

_____

8. A waiter offered mints *to the diners*.

_____

9. I bought tickets *for the entire family*!

_____

10. William e-mailed a funny message *to Jack*.

_____

Composition Hint

Certain verbs are frequently used in sentences with indirect objects. Here are some of those verbs:

bring	buy	give
hand	lend	make
offer	pay	promise
send	tell	write

 Writing
Application

Using Indirect and Direct Objects

Choose **five** verbs from the box above and use each one to write a sentence containing an indirect object and a direct object. Write your sentences on a separate sheet of paper and underline and label each object as *direct* or *indirect*.

Combine the two-letter blocks to form nouns of four letters. Use each block only once. Then, on the lines provided, use each noun as a direct object or an indirect object in a sentence. One item is completed for you as a sample.

Hint: Only one word starts with a vowel.

Things You Find in a Kitchen

DI	OV
SI	
OD	SH	KE
DO	R K	SO
LK	CO	
	NK	
F O	LT	
OK		MI
EN	CA	
AP	FO	
OR	SA	

FORK

1. _____
2. _____
3. _____
4. _____
5. _____
6. _____
7. _____
8. _____
9. _____
10. _____

11. _____

12. _____

13. _____

14. _____

15. _____

16. _____

17. _____

18. _____

19. _____

20. _____

7 Pronouns and Antecedents

 A *pronoun* takes the place of a noun.

QUESTION 1: How many pronouns are in the following sentence?

Jeffrey wrote a poem, and he called it "Faded Freedom."

ANSWER: Two.

He is a pronoun taking the place of the noun *Jeffrey*.

It is a pronoun taking the place of the noun *poem*.

QUESTION 2: What is an *antecedent*?

ANSWER: **An *antecedent* is the noun that a pronoun stands for.**

In the sentence above, the antecedent of the pronoun *he* is the noun *Jeffrey*. The antecedent of the pronoun *it* is the noun *poem*.

QUESTION 3: Why are pronouns important?

ANSWER: Pronouns make language more smooth and efficient because they let us express ourselves without repetition and with fewer words. If there were no pronouns, we would have to say,

Jeffrey wrote a poem, and Jeffrey called the poem "Faded Freedom."

Here are more examples of pronouns and antecedents in sentences.

Happily, the *goldfish* swam in its bowl.

Majestic *mountains* cast their shadows across the valley.

Veronica glanced impatiently at her watch.

Although *Corbin* hadn't met the new *neighbors,* he waved at them.

ACTIVITY 1

Underline each pronoun. Then draw an arrow from the pronoun to its antecedent.

> **Sample:**
>
> Herbert, where is your project for the science fair?

1. Kathy accidentally broke her arm during spring break.

2. Unfortunately, Ted's favorite lamp has a crack in its base.

3. Ms. Pulaski lost the keys but later found them.

4. Eagerly, Jamaal wrote down his ideas for earning money.

5. The turtles found themselves a warm rock in the sun.

ACTIVITY 2

Each sentence has two pronouns and two antecedents. Underline each pronoun. Then draw an arrow from the pronoun to its antecedent.

> **Sample:**
>
> The e-mails made the journalist smile when she read them.

1. Lyle painted his walls blue, but Cindy painted hers yellow.

2. Erin, find your way to the sink—the dishes won't wash themselves.

3. The ice cools the sodas, but it makes them watery, too.

4. If the bees find the new flowers, they will love them.

5. The gardener was glad when ladybugs made their home on her rosebush.

ACTIVITY 3

In the blank space, write a pronoun that refers to the italicized antecedent.

> **Samples:**
>
> **a.** *Alexander Graham Bell* spoke to _____his_____ assistant on a telegraph line.
>
> **b.** Civil rights *supporters* raised _____their_____ voices against segregation.

1. The *Philadelphia Zoo* opened _____its_____ doors in 1874.

2. *Alaskans* know that _____their_____ state is the largest in the nation.

3. Most *victims* of the bubonic plague did not know what had made _____them_____ ill.

4. The *Titanic* was poorly equipped; _____it_____ didn't have enough lifeboats.

5. *General George Washington* expected _____his_____ orders to be obeyed.

6. Some *pioneers* built homes for _____themselves_____ out of sod (dirt).

7. In the 1850s, *Amelia Bloomer* wore loose pants under _____her_____ skirts.

8. People laughed at the *pants* and called _____them_____ "bloomers."

9. *Robert E. Peary* took dogs with _____him_____ to the North Pole.

10. The honeysuckle *blossom* has a sweet-tasting nectar in _____it_____.

Writing Application

Using Pronouns and Antecedents

Write your name at the top of a sheet of paper. With your teacher's approval, follow these steps:

(1) Write **one** sentence that uses a noun as a subject.

(2) Pass the paper to the person sitting behind you.

(3) Read the sentence you receive, and write a new sentence using a pronoun to refer to the subject of the first sentence.

(4) Write a new sentence using a new noun as a subject.

(5) Pass the paper to the person behind you.

(6) Continue with the process until you have used pronouns in **five** sentences.

(7) Retrieve the paper with your name on it, and read what people have written.

Composition Hint

Every pronoun should *clearly* refer to an antecedent, either in the same sentence or in a sentence that came before.

UNCLEAR: When *Marta* first met *Sabrina,* she was ten years old.

(Who was ten years old, Marta or Sabrina?)

CLEAR: *Marta* was ten years old when she first met Sabrina.

CLEAR: When she first met Sabrina, *Marta* was ten years old.

UNCLEAR: *Oliver* became friends with *Roberto* in the fifth grade. That year, each student was assigned a different "study buddy" for each six-week grading period. When the first buddies were assigned, he was delighted. Even after the six-week period was over, he remained loyal to his new friend.

(Do the pronouns refer to Oliver or Roberto?)

CLEAR: *Oliver* became friends with *Roberto* in the fifth grade. That year, each student was assigned a different "study buddy" for each six-week grading period. When the first buddies were assigned, Roberto was delighted. Even after the six-week period was over, he remained loyal to his new friend.

(To clarify whom the pronouns refer to, the relevant noun, *Roberto,* must be restated.)

Revise the following paragraph so that each pronoun refers clearly to its antecedent. Write your revision on the lines provided. Circle each pronoun and draw an arrow from it to its antecedent.

> **Sample:**
>
> When fans of the Hawks looked across the court at the Stallions' fans, they began chanting, "We're the team that can't be beat! Just drop right down and kiss our feet!"
>
> _When fans of the Hawks looked across the court at the Stallions' fans, the Hawks began chanting, "We are the team that can't be beat! Just drop right down and kiss our feet!"_

In the playoffs, the Hawks beat the Stallions by only two points. The team was at its best at that point in the season, and its fans packed the stands to see the players show what they could do. When the final play was made, and the Hawks were named the champions, fans cheered as they waved victoriously.

_____

_____

_____

_____

_____

_____

Personal Pronouns

 The _personal pronouns_ are I, you, he, she, it, we, they.

These are called _personal_ pronouns because, except for _it,_ they all refer to _persons._ These pronouns are among the most troublesome words in our language.

QUESTION: Why are the personal pronouns troublesome?

ANSWER: Most of these pronouns change form, depending on how they are used in a sentence. On the other hand, the nouns that these pronouns stand for do not change.

For example, take the noun _Kristy._ We can use _Kristy_ as a subject, a direct object, or an indirect object.

SUBJECT:	Kristy laughed.
	S. V.

DIRECT OBJECT:	The joke amused Kristy.
	S. V. D.O.

INDIRECT OBJECT:	The joke gave Kristy a smile.
	S. V. I.O. D.O.

Obviously, the noun *Kristy* does not change form, whether it is used as a subject, a direct object, or an indirect object.

But most pronouns change form, depending on their use. For example, *she* can be used as a subject but not as a direct object or indirect object. Take a look at the example sentences again, this time with pronouns used in place of *Kristy*.

SUBJECT:	She laughed.
	S. V.

DIRECT OBJECT:	The joke amused her.
	S. V. D.O.

INDIRECT OBJECT:	The joke gave her a smile.
	S. V. I.O. D.O.

ACTIVITY 5

In the blank space, use a personal pronoun in place of the italicized antecedent.

Sample:

> *Denzel* said, "_____I_____ love this song!"

1. When *Jason* got to the park, _____ fed the pigeons.

2. *Diana and Carlos* need sunscreen if _____ will be outdoors.

3. Rosemary got bitten by an *ant* and then squashed _____.

4. *Uncle Elroy*, do _____ know how to fly an airplane?

5. Before *Hannah* dove in, _____ tested the water's temperature.

The Different Forms of the Personal Pronouns

If we need a pronoun as a SUBJECT, we can use one of the following:

I	you	he	she	it	we	they

If we need a pronoun as a DIRECT OBJECT or INDIRECT OBJECT, we can use one of these:

me	you	him	her	it	us	them

If we need a pronoun to show POSSESSION, we can use one of these:

my	your	his	her	its	our	their
mine	yours		hers		ours	theirs

Note: Only *you* and *it* have the same form for subject, direct object, and indirect object.

Supply the missing pronoun.

> **Samples:**
>
> **a.** The canaries are hungry. Please give _____them_____ some seeds.
>
> **b.** Frannie paid for the birthstone ring. It is officially _____hers_____.

1. Edgar Allan Poe is an American poet. _____ wrote "The Raven."

2. Yasmin and Dion are vegetarians, so give _____ vegetable plates.

3. The mother bear is very protective of _____ cubs.

4. This science project is mine. Ken, where is _____?

5. Jinny and I love books, so _____ started a book club together.

6. I love it when friends send _____ e-mails or text messages.

7. This accident was caused by Sally. Everyone blames _____.

8. My family lives in this building. This is _____ door.

9. We got our invitation, but did the Crenshaws get _____?

10. Clark needs to write a book report. Please lend _____ a novel.

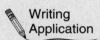 Writing
Application

Using Personal Pronouns

Every generation of students encounters a slightly different set of banned books. *Brave New World, Invisible Man, To Kill a Mockingbird, A Light in the Attic*—these and many, many more have been objected to or banned outright in some schools. Do you think banning students' access to books is justifiable? Do you think others in your class agree with you?

Interview a classmate about his or her opinions on banning books. The two of you may or may not share the same opinions. Then, on a separate sheet of paper, write a paragraph of **seven** or more sentences explaining what you and your classmate each think about the banning of books. Use at least **five** different personal pronouns and circle each one.

Agreement of Pronoun and Antecedent

A pronoun should *agree* with its antecedent in two ways.

1. The pronoun and antecedent should agree in _gender_ (male, female, or neuter).

MALE   MALE
Stephen King wrote the final paragraph of *his* new novel.

2. The pronoun and antecedent should agree in _number_ (singular or plural).

PLURAL   PLURAL
Readers say *they* enjoy King's novels.

Here are more examples of pronouns that agree with their antecedents.

Bill carried the petition with *him*.

(The antecedent *Bill* is masculine and singular. The pronoun *him* is masculine and singular. They agree.)

The *princess* smiled *her* brightest smile.

(The antecedent *princess* is feminine and singular. The pronoun *her* is feminine and singular. They agree.)

The two *rivers* wind *their* way through town.

(The antecedent *rivers* is neuter and plural. The pronoun *their* is plural and can be used with any gender antecedent. They agree.)

If you do not know the gender of a singular antecedent, use a form of the *he or she* construction to refer to the antecedent.

GENDER?   MALE OR FEMALE

A *student* who turns in *his or her* report early will get extra credit.

Another way to keep the gender neutral is to change the sentence to plural form.

Students who turn in *their* reports early will get extra credit.

ACTIVITY 7

Underline the antecedent in each sentence. Then underline the correct pronoun to use with the antecedent.

Samples:

a. My younger <u>sisters</u> expect me to play with (*her*, *them*).

b. If a <u>hiker</u> gets lost, (*he or she*, *they*) should stay in one place and wait.

1. Several rabbits made (*its, their*) home in the thicket.

2. Aunt Roxy loves boxing, and (*she, they*) watches it on TV.

3. Rutherford insisted that everyone call (*it, him*) Rusty.

4. The paper cups were empty, so (*it, they*) blew in the wind.

5. Each morning, Mr. Caruso combs (*his, her*) mustache.

6. The parrot likes to have a mirror in (*their, its*) cage.

7. Marlon meant well, but (*he, it*) made things worse.

8. A writer must proofread (*their, his or her*) work carefully.

9. Emily raised (*her, their*) hand immediately.

10. If that old door were painted, (*it, they*) would look much better.

Pronouns in Combinations

Pronouns and nouns may be combined to form compound subjects, compound indirect objects, and compound objects.

COMPOUND SUBJECT: *Brenda and I* went swimming.

COMPOUND INDIRECT OBJECT: Mom gave *Brenda and me* fresh towels.

COMPOUND DIRECT OBJECT: The water refreshed *Brenda and me*.

Composition Hint

Make your writing more interesting and effective by removing unnecessary words. Note how compound subjects, compound direct objects, and compound indirect objects can help.

INSTEAD OF: My friends live near a park. I live near a park.

WRITE: *My friends and I* live near a park. (compound subject)

INSTEAD OF: The scary movie frightened Felix. The movie frightened her.

WRITE: The scary movie frightened *Felix and her*. (compound direct object)

INSTEAD OF: Give Mr. Morris your money. Give them your money.

WRITE: Give *Mr. Morris or them* your money. (compound indirect object)

ACTIVITY 8

Rewrite each pair of sentences as one sentence, taking out the unnecessary words. Your new sentence should contain a compound subject, compound indirect object, or compound direct object. Circle the compound element and label it.

Samples:

a. The neighbors hosted the barbecue. We hosted the barbecue, too.

Compound subject

The neighbors and we hosted the barbecue.

b. Please reserve Shelley a table. Please reserve me a table.

Compound indirect object

Please reserve Shelley and me a table.

1. She organized a fund-raiser. The staff organized the fund-raiser, too.

_____

2. Stanley photographed Duke. Stanley also photographed me.

_____

3. The college sent Stephanie a catalog. The college sent me a catalog.

_____

4. You should wash it with soap. You should also wash the dress with soap.

_____

5. The class walked to the auditorium. He also walked to the auditorium.

_____

Writing Application

Using Pronouns and Antecedents

Brainstorm a list of **ten** nouns that help paint a word picture of who you are. Examples are *art, books, computers, race cars, fashion, pets, dance,* and so on. Write a paragraph explaining why **five** of these help define you. Underline each pronoun and make sure it agrees with its antecedent.

Pronouns in Contractions

As we noted in Lesson 3, page 29,

 A *contraction* is a combination of two words with one or more letters omitted.

 An *apostrophe* ['] takes the place of the omitted letters.

Pronouns can form contractions with verbs.

PRONOUN	+	VERB	=	CONTRACTION	LETTER(S) OMITTED
you	+	are	=	*you're*	a
they	+	have	=	*they've*	ha
she	+	will	=	*she'll*	wi

Note that the first word in a contraction does not lose any letters—only the second word does. In the contraction *let's,* the pronoun *us* loses a letter because it is the second word.

let	+	us	=	*let's*

Contractions are commonly used in conversation and friendly letters and notes. Here are examples of pronoun contractions we frequently use:

it	+	is	=	*it's*
she	+	will	=	*she'll*
they	+	will	=	*they'll*
they	+	have	=	*they've*
you	+	have	=	*you've*
I	+	am	=	*I'm*

we	+	are	=	*we're*
he	+	would	=	*he'd*
they	+	would	=	*they'd*
you	+	are	=	*you're*
they	+	are	=	*they're*

ACTIVITY 9

A contraction stands for two words. Write the two words for each italicized contraction below.

> **Sample:**
>
> *They'd* like it. = _____They would_____

1. *He'll* be there. = _____

2. *She'd* enjoy that. = _____

3. *We've* arrived. = _____

4. *Let's* play ball! = _____

5. *You're* funny. = _____

CAUTION: Do not confuse a contraction with a possessive pronoun.

A contraction *always* has an apostrophe.

you're (you are); *it's* (it is)

A possessive pronoun *never* has an apostrophe.

your, his, hers, its, ours, theirs

CONTRACTIONS

(Use an apostrophe to replace omitted letters.)

It's (It is) broken.

You're (You are) pretty.

They're (They are) playing.

POSSESSIVE PRONOUNS

(Do not use an apostrophe.)

Its surface is dusty.

Your locker is open.

Their team won.

ACTIVITY 10

Write the choice that makes the sentence correct.

> **Samples:**
>
> **a.** (*It's, Its*) not where I left it. _____It's_____
>
> **b.** No one can read (*you're, your*) handwriting. _____your_____

1. (*It's, Its*) not my fault! _____

2. This treasure chest is (*our's, ours*). _____

3. The trees are losing (*they're, their*) leaves. _____

4. I'm sorry that (*you're, your*) upset. _____

5. That empty desk is (*her's, hers*). _____

6. (*They're, Their*) late again. _____

7. (*Let's, Lets*) be friends. _____

8. I like (*you're, your*) haircut. _____

9. Is the tennis racquet Dave's or (*our's, ours*)? _____

10. The cat licked (*it's, its*) whiskers. _____

ACTIVITY 11

Each block below contains a personal pronoun. Decide the form of each pronoun (subject, object, or possessive). Then write the pronoun in the correct column. Use each block only once. One item is completed as a sample.

we	our	she	me	her	their	it
his	him	them	they	I	her	~~you~~
it	you	its	your	us	he	my

Subject	Object	Possessive
you		

Review of Verbs, Nouns, and Pronouns

To learn what part of speech a word is, ask yourself: How is the word used in its sentence?

For example, in sentence 1 below, *water* is a noun; it names a thing. In sentence 2, *water* is a verb; it expresses action.

1. Cool <u>water</u> is refreshing.
      N.

2. Please <u>water</u> the plants.
      V.

Study these additional examples:

NOUN: Ouch! I burned my <u>hand</u>.

          (*Hand* names a thing.)

VERB: Please <u>hand</u> me that notebook.

          (*Hand* expresses an action.)

NOUN: Which <u>seat</u> would you prefer?

          (*Seat* names a thing.)

VERB: I <u>will seat</u> the guests at the table.

          (*Will seat* expresses an action.)

ACTIVITY 1

Unscramble each word, using the hints provided. Next, write two sentences for each word—first, use the word as a verb, then use the word as a noun. One item is completed as a sample.

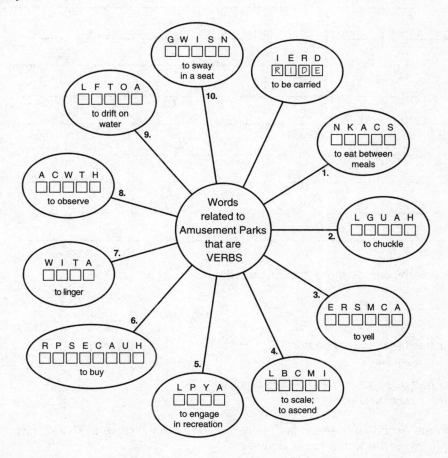

1. *verb:* _____

   noun: _____

2. *verb:* _____

   noun: _____

3. *verb:* _____

   noun: _____

4. *verb:* _____

   noun: _____

5. *verb:* _____

   noun: _____

6. *verb:* _____

   noun: _____

7. *verb:* _____

   noun: _____

8. *verb:* _____

   noun: _____

9. *verb:* _____

   noun: _____

10. *verb:* _____

    noun: _____

Remember that verbs can be more than one word.

The carpenter *sawed* boards.
    VERB

The carpenter *has been sawing* boards.
    VERB PHRASE

The carpenter *has been sawing and nailing* boards.
    COMPOUND VERB

Whenever you are asked for the verb in a sentence, *give the whole verb.* That is, give the whole verb phrase or the whole compound verb.

ACTIVITY 2

Write the verb in each sentence.

> **Samples:**
>
> **a.** They should have already been warned. _should have been warned_
>
> **b.** Doesn't the doll talk or sing? _Does talk or sing_

1. The patient must have forgotten his appointment. _____

2. Have the midterms been graded? _____

3. White curtains flapped in the breeze. _____

4. Who was using this computer? _____

5. She doesn't want our pity. _____

6. I had showered and dressed by six A.M. _____

7. Keep the jeans but toss the old shoes. _____

8. Without water, he would have soon fainted. _____

9. The flight might have just been delayed. _____

10. Don't you know me better than that? _____

The subject of a sentence may be one word, a compound noun, or a compound subject.

The *carpenter* sawed boards. (One word)

The *construction worker* sawed boards. (Compound noun)

The *carpenter and construction worker* sawed boards. (Compound subject)

Whenever you are asked for the subject in a sentence, *give the whole subject*. That is, give the whole compound noun or the whole compound subject.

ACTIVITY 3

Write the subject in each sentence.

> **Samples:**
>
> **a.** Does Great-Grandpa or his friend drive? _Great-Grandpa or friend_
>
> **b.** The great white shark is magnificent. _great white shark_

1. My brother-in-law phoned last night. _____

2. The bass guitar and cello are great instruments. _____

3. Did Arturo or Amy attend school today? _____

4. The potatoes, leeks, and onions go in the soup. _____

5. Mount Rushmore is a popular tourist attraction. _____

6. His self-esteem and confidence are both high. _____

7. Please lock the door and turn off the lights. _____

8. Didn't Professor Chang or Kris tell you? _____

9. Flat stones or a footbridge would work. _____

10. Fedoras, sombreros, and bowlers are hats. _____

As you have learned, a pronoun can take the place of a noun. Nouns and pronouns can be used as subjects, as direct objects, as indirect objects, or to show possession.

Damion bought *me* a *wallet*. *His* gift was generous.
S.   I.O.   D.O. POSS.

An antecedent is the word for which a pronoun stands. In the sentence above, the noun *Damion* is the antecedent of the pronoun *His*.

ACTIVITY 4 _____

Write the part of speech of each underlined word (verb, noun, or pronoun). Then write how it is used in the sentence. You may use these abbreviations:

verb (V.)	action verb (action)	linking verb (linking)
noun (N.)	subject (Subj.)	direct object (D.O.)
pronoun (P.)	indirect object (I.O.)	possessive (Poss.)

Samples:

	PART OF SPEECH	HOW USED
a. Household rules <u>can feel</u> restrictive.	verb	linking
b. In fact, teenagers should set their own <u>rules</u>.	noun	D.O.

	PART OF SPEECH	HOW USED
1. <u>Have</u> you ever <u>disobeyed</u> your parents?	_____	_____
2. For example, <u>they</u> tell you, "No television tonight."	_____	_____
3. Then Jeremiah invites you over to <u>his</u> house.	_____	_____
4. You and Jeremiah watch <u>television</u> all evening.	_____	_____
5. They <u>declare</u>, "No parties while we're gone."	_____	_____
6. "My life <u>is</u> homework," you reply.	_____	_____

7. The <u>invitations</u> go out that very day. _____ _____

8. Dad says, "<u>Don't</u> <u>drive</u> the car without me." _____ _____

9. You give the <u>car</u> a quick spin. _____ _____

10. Naturally, a cop pulls <u>you</u> over for speeding. _____ _____

ACTIVITY 5 _____

Read the recipe for microwave nachos. Underline each noun <u>once</u>, and each verb <u>twice</u>. Then circle each pronoun and draw an arrow from the pronoun to its antecedent.

> **Samples:**
>
> **a.** <u>Nachos</u> <u>can be</u> a healthy <u>snack</u>.
>
> **b.** <u>Prepare</u> this <u>dish</u> in a <u>hurry</u> and <u>enjoy</u> (it) with <u>friends</u>.

COUNTDOWN TO MICROWAVE NACHOS

10. Open a bag of plain tortilla chips.

9. Shred some cheese, about 1/2 cup.

8. Wash a small tomato and dice it up.

7. Slice jalapeños (hot peppers), or open a can of them.

6. Open a container of sour cream.

5. Spread the tortilla chips on a microwave-safe plate.

4. Sprinkle the cheese evenly over the chips.

3. Microwave on high heat 30 to 45 seconds, or until the cheese is melted.

2. Remove the plate from the microwave; put tomatoes and jalapeños on top.

1. Enjoy! Serve hot, with a dollop of sour cream on the side.

Recall that in less formal writing and conversation, contractions may be used.

ACTIVITY 6 _____

Which contraction *beginning with a pronoun* can replace the italicized words in each sentence? Write your answer on the line provided.

> **Samples:**
>
> **a.** Sure, *we would* love to attend. _____we'd_____
>
> **b.** *Bill* and *Beth Riley are* honest people. _____They're_____

1. *You have* made a good first impression. _____

2. Soon, *Dan will* solve the riddle. _____

3. *The library books are* overdue. _____

4. Yes, *she will* meet you at the flagpoles. _____

5. *The calculator* is solar-powered. _____

6. Of course *my friends would* love this place. _____

7. Whew! *We have* worked really hard. _____

8. Earlier *Maria had* caused a commotion. _____

9. I *would* enjoy going running with you. _____

10. Lynn, *you are* a loyal friend. _____

For Activities 7–10, read the following excerpt from "Lot No. 249," a short story by Arthur Conan Doyle.

It moved in the shadow of the hedge, silently and furtively, a dark crouching figure, dimly visible against the black background. Even as he gazed back at it, it had lessened its distance by twenty <u>paces</u>, and was fast closing in on him. Out of the darkness he had a glimpse of a scraggy neck, and of two eyes that will ever haunt him in his dreams. He turned, and with a cry of terror he ran for his life up the avenue. . . . He was a famous runner, but never had he run as he ran that night.

. . . As he rushed madly and wildly through the night he could hear a swift dry patter behind him, and could see, as he threw back a glance, that this horror was bounding like a tiger at his heels, with blazing eyes and stringy arms outthrown. . . . Nearer yet sounded the clatter from <u>behind</u>. He heard a hoarse gurgling at his very shoulder. With a shriek he flung himself against the door, slammed and bolted it behind him, and sank half-fainting onto the hall chair.

ACTIVITY 7 _____

Use the passage to do each of these tasks:

1. Underline each noun in the two paragraphs. There are 32 nouns in all, including the two that are already underlined as samples.

2. As you have learned, nouns can be either common or proper. Which kind of noun is used in this passage? _____

3. In the passage, certain words that Doyle uses as nouns can also be used as verbs. These words are *shadow, hedge, figure, paces, glimpse, eyes, dreams, cry, patter, glance, heels, clatter, gurgling, shoulder, shriek,* and *chair.* Choose three of these words and use them as verbs in sentences on the following lines. In each sentence, circle the word you are using as a verb.

a. _____

b. _____

c. _____

ACTIVITY 8

Use the passage to do each of these tasks:

1. Doyle uses five different pronouns in these two paragraphs. List them here:

_____ _____ _____ _____ _____

2. Use each pronoun you listed in item 1 to write a sentence of your own.

a. _____

b. _____

c. _____

d. _____

e. _____

ACTIVITY 9

This excerpt begins with the pronoun *it*. In the story, Doyle does not provide an antecedent for *it*, although he does use *Abercrombie Smith* earlier in the story as the antecedent of *he*. Why do you think Doyle does not use a specific noun to identify *it*? Write your answer in complete sentences on the lines below.

_____

_____

_____

_____

_____

Why do you think Doyle does not use contractions in the passage? Write your answer in complete sentences on the lines below.

_____

_____

_____

Verbs, Nouns, and Pronouns

It's time to take a break from traditional grammar exercises. The following activities ask you to explore how people use verbs, nouns, and pronouns in the real world, outside your classroom walls. Which activity sparks your interest? Choose an activity to complete; then, with your teacher's approval, share the results with your classmates. Have a good time!

The Spice of Life

Variety is the spice of life. When it comes to discussing sports, a variety of **verbs** can add a lot of flavor. Watch a sporting event and then write up the event in one page or less. Underline each verb. Now add the spice. In a thesaurus, find alternatives for overused or bland verbs. For example, does one team *win*, or does it *trounce* the competition? Add the new "spicy" verbs to your write-up. Show both versions to a friend or your classmates and ask which is more powerful.

Game Show Host

Host a trivia game for your class. Choose five categories (famous cities, musicians, U.S. states, etc.). On index cards, write short descriptions of two examples from each category using **pronouns** and **common nouns** instead of **proper nouns.** At the bottom of each card, for your eyes only, write the proper noun being described. Divide your class into small groups. Announce each category and read a description from that category. The first group to guess the proper noun wins a point. The group that accumulates the most points wins.

"Mailman" or "Mail Carrier"?

Some **nouns** are considered sexist—that is, they exclude women by their very structure, as in fireman and mankind. Likewise, some uses of **pronouns** are considered sexist, such as using *he* to refer to an antecedent that could mean *he* or *she*. What is your opinion of so-called sexist language? Why do you think it's considered inappropriate? Give examples of sexist language and explain if and/or how you would revise each example.

Time Capsule

Make a time capsule to open in ten years. Include small mementos, photos, and a summary of life today. To write the summary, make a list of **common nouns.** Then expand on each common noun by listing related **proper nouns** that are significant today. Seal everything in a shoe box or other container, with a note on the lid stating when it is to be opened.

Surfing for Knowledge

Choose to work with one of the following: (1) subjects and predicates, (2) verbs, (3) nouns, or (4) pronouns and antecedents. Your task? Survey five educational sites on the Internet that relate to your topic. Evaluate each site for accuracy, clarity, thoroughness, and one or two other qualities of your choice. Type up a report listing the Web sites and your evaluation of each. Be sure to state what visitors to each site can expect to learn. With your teacher's approval, post your report in the classroom, or pass out copies.

9 Adjectives

What is the difference between *backpack* and *the old canvas backpack*?

Backpack means any backpack at all. The words *the, old,* and *canvas* **modify** (change) the meaning of *backpack* from any backpack to one particular backpack. These words that make nouns more rich, varied, and clear are *adjectives.*

 An *adjective* is a word that modifies a noun or a pronoun.

ADJECTIVES: Turn down the *loud* music.

I'd love a *cold* soda.

The band is *excellent.*

QUESTION: Are the words *a, an* and *the* adjectives?

ANSWER: Yes, the words *a, an* and *the* are the most frequently used of all adjectives. They are called **articles**. Since they appear so often, we will exclude them (ignore them) when identifying adjectives in this book.

Adjectives give information by answering such questions as *What kind? Which one? How many? Whose?*

WHAT KIND? *hot* water, *smelly* socks, *white* flower

WHICH ONE? *that* building, *third* request, *favorite* class

HOW MANY? *five* fingers, *several* assignments, *many* ideas

WHOSE? *our* plan, *her* desk, *my* property

QUESTION: In the examples above, why are the words *that, several,* and *many* called adjectives? Aren't these words pronouns?

ANSWER: A word's part of speech depends on how the word is used. In the examples above, *that, several,* and *many* are used as adjectives to modify nouns.

Compare these examples:

ADJECTIVE: Trumaine's office is inside *that* building. (*That* modifies *building.*)

PRONOUN: *That* is Trumaine's office. (*That* is used as the subject of the sentence.)

ADJECTIVE: Penelope must complete *several* assignments tonight. (*Several* modifies *assignments.*)

PRONOUN: I helped her with *several.* (*Several* is used as the object of the preposition *with.*)

Study the following list of words that may be used either as adjectives or pronouns. Then as you do the activities in this book, pay special attention to how these words are used in sentences.

this	any	most
that	enough	much
these	few	several
those	many	some

ACTIVITY 1 _____

Each sentence contains one adjective. Underline the adjective and draw an arrow from the adjective to the noun or pronoun it modifies.

> **Sample:**
>
> I'd like a <u>few</u> copies, please.

1. Annabeth likes the green ones.

2. Did you feel welcome?

3. His gloves have been lost.

4. Don't make me wear the frilly shirt!

5. They were generous.

6. This one was broken during shipping.

7. At the wooden gate, turn left.

8. I'm asking for the last time.

9. In fact, she had become reclusive.

10. We listened to soft music.

QUESTION: Can a sentence have more than one adjective?

ANSWER: Yes. The number of adjectives can vary from zero to many, depending on what the writer needs to say.

The following sentence contains five adjectives.

A *strong* hurricane washed *muddy* debris onto the *sandy* beach while *several* lifeguards watched from *safe* shelters.

Now read the same sentence without its adjectives.

A hurricane washed debris onto the beach while lifeguards watched from shelters.

How has the sentence changed?

Placement of Adjectives

An adjective often comes before the word it modifies. Study these examples:

1. The *busy lifeguards* needed a rest.

   (NOT The *lifeguards busy* needed a rest.)

2. *Happy children* splashed in the water.

   (NOT *Children happy* splashed in the water.)

In some cases, an adjective follows the word it modifies. Usually, the sentence follows the pattern of subject + linking verb + adjective.

The examples below demonstrate this pattern.

3. The lifeguards were *busy*.
   SUBJ.   L.V.   ADJ.

4. Children in the water felt *happy*.
   SUBJ.   L.V. ADJ.

ACTIVITY 2

Each sentence contains two or more adjectives. Underline each adjective, and draw an arrow from the adjective to the noun or pronoun it modifies. (Remember, do not include articles.)

Sample:

One late night I was hungry for chocolate ice cream.

1. I grabbed my fuzzy sweater and borrowed the blue pickup.

2. For a whole year, I had been driving the short distance to the store.

3. That particular night, however, I became unsure of the proper route.

4. At the first corner I turned, guiding my trusty truck along the straight boulevard.

5. After I passed an old warehouse, I realized I was on the wrong road.

6. Immediately, I looked for a memorable landmark or a familiar street.

7. I was crestfallen to realize these avenues did not spark a tiny memory.

8. At this point, there was one thing to do.

9. I pulled into the bright lot of a small store and whipped out my cell phone.

10. Quickly I punched in an important number and let out a loud whine: "Mooooommmm! I need help!"

Writing Application

Using Adjectives

When was the last time you desperately needed someone's help? On a separate sheet of paper, write **two** paragraphs of at least **five** sentences each describing the situation and the type of help you needed. Explain how a particular person came to your aid and how that made you feel. Use at least **ten** adjectives in your paragraphs and underline each one.

Composition Hint

Adjectives can make your writing come alive. Think about having lunch in the school cafeteria, or watching an action movie on television. In order to describe either of these experiences to a friend, you would probably use several adjectives to make your description clear and vivid. Compare these two sentence pairs:

WITHOUT ADJECTIVES: The room was filled with smells and students.

WITH ADJECTIVES: The sunny room was filled with *delicious* smells and *hungry* students.

WITHOUT ADJECTIVES: That movie had special effects and a plot.

WITH ADJECTIVES: That movie had *disappointing* special effects and a *boring* plot.

ACTIVITY 3

Rewrite each sentence using one or more adjectives to make each noun more specific.

> **Sample:**
>
> The fisherman held up a fish.
>
> *The proud fisherman held up a fat fish.*

1. The game ended with a touchdown.

   _____

2. You should wear the shirt and tie.

   _____

3. A volcano poured lava on the town.

   _____

4. Would you like a sandwich and drink?

   _____

5. The teacher gave an assignment to the students.

   _____

Writing Application

Using Adjectives to Make Writing Clear and Vivid

Using the sentences in Activity 3 as examples, write **five** sentences **without** adjectives. Write your sentences on a separate sheet of paper and, with your teacher's approval, exchange sentences with a classmate. Rewrite each of your classmate's sentences, making them more clear and vivid by adding adjectives. Share the results with your classmate.

ACTIVITY 4 _____

Rearrange the letters on each license plate to form an adjective. Then use each adjective in a sentence of your own. One item is completed as a sample.

Hint: Each adjective can be used to describe a car.

California		ILLINOIS		COLORADO	
OEN-DRM	1.	UUF-LES	2.	STO·PYR	

New York		TEXAS		WYOMING	
EPYSDE		YS NIH		OLC-TYS	
3.		4.		5.	

Sample:

a. _____ modern _____

b. _____ Do you like modern cars or classic ones better? _____

1. a. _____

   b. _____

2. a. _____

   b. _____

3. a. _____

   b. _____

4. a. _____

   b. _____

5. a. _____

   b. _____

Some words may be used as either an adjective or a noun.

ADJECTIVE: *Orange* cones marked the work zone. (*Orange* modifies the noun *cones*.)

NOUN: A juicy *orange* makes a good snack. (*Orange* names a fruit. It is the subject of the sentence.)

ADJECTIVE: Please refill the *water* bottles. (*Water* modifies the noun bottles.)

NOUN: Would you like some *water*? (*Water* names a thing. It is the direct object of the verb *Would like*.)

ACTIVITY 5

Look at the italicized word. If it is used as a noun, write *N* on the line provided. If it is used as an adjective, write *Adj*.

Samples:

  Adj   **a.** Many *desert* animals rest during the day.

  _N_   **b.** The sandfish (a type of lizard) lives in the *desert*.

1. _____ **a.** Please pass me the *strawberry* jam.

_____ **b.** When ripe, the *strawberry* is juicy and red.

2. _____ **a.** Ouch! I stubbed my bare toe on a *stone*.

_____ **b.** A *stone* wall divides the courtyard from the street.

3. _____ **a.** Luckily, the *school* has several large parking lots.

_____ **b.** The *school* parking lot is for faculty, staff, and students.

4. _____ **a.** Slowly, a road grader leveled the *country* road.

_____ **b.** Honduras is a Central American *country* that lies north of Nicaragua.

5. _____ **a.** For the party, I set out *paper* napkins and plastic forks.

_____ **b.** Use plain white *paper* for typing the memo.

Proper Adjectives

Recall that proper nouns (*America, Shakespeare,* etc.) are capitalized. The adjectives formed from proper nouns (*American, Shakespearean*) are capitalized, too. They are called **proper adjectives**. Here are some proper nouns and the proper adjectives that can be formed from them.

PROPER NOUN	PROPER ADJECTIVE
Africa	*African* country
Texas	*Texan* tradition
Freud	*Freudian* psychologist
Democrat	*Democratic* voter
Mars	*Martian* landscape

Some proper nouns do not change form when they are used as a proper adjective. You must look at how the word is used in the sentence to decide if it is a proper noun or proper adjective.

PROPER NOUN	PROPER ADJECTIVE
New England	New England countryside
Brooklyn	Brooklyn accent

ACTIVITY 6

Underline the proper adjective in each sentence. Then draw an arrow from the adjective to the noun or pronoun it modifies.

Sample:

The lucky winner received a <u>Hawaiian</u> vacation.

1. At the museum, the class studied Italian paintings.

2. Has Melinda ever been to the Maine coast?

3. That is a lovely Persian rug in your den!

4. In theory, the practice of Marxist principles should lead to a classless society.

5. Which Japanese car is your favorite?

ESL Focus

Forming Adjectives from Nouns

In English, certain suffixes are often used to make proper adjectives out of proper nouns. (A *suffix* is a word part added to the end of a word to create a new word.) Study the following suffixes, meanings, and examples.

SUFFIX	MEANING	EXAMPLE
-an, -ean, -ian	one who, one that	*African:* one that originates in Africa
-ese	relating to, originating in	*Japanese:* one who originates in Japan
-ic, -iac	like, relating to	*Democratic:* relating to a Democrat
-ist	one who, relating to	*Marxist:* one who follows Marx

To make an adjective out of the noun *north, south, east,* or *west,* we add *–ern.* The adjective forms are *northern, southern, eastern,* and *western.*

Add each suffix to the proper noun it follows to form a proper adjective. Then use the adjective to modify a noun.

NOUN	+	SUFFIX	=	ADJECTIVE

Samples:

a. West   + -ern   =   *Western medicine*

b. Buddha + -ist   =   *Buddhist teachings*

1. South America + -an   = _____

2. Elizabeth + -an   = _____

3. China + -ese   = _____

4. Brazil + -ian   = _____

5. Victoria + -an   = _____

6. East + -ern   = _____

7. California + -an   = _____

8. Jefferson + -ian   = _____

9. Darwin + -ian   = _____

10. Shakespeare + -an   = _____

Writing Application

Using Proper Adjectives

Imagine that you are opening a brand new pizza parlor called Pizzas of the World. Each pizza on your menu features toppings from a different place in the world—for example, a continent such as Africa, a nation such as Italy, or a state such as Hawaii.

On a separate sheet of paper, write a menu for your restaurant, listing **ten** different pizzas with descriptions of their toppings. Use at least one proper adjective in each pizza's name or description. Underline each common adjective <u>once</u>, and underline each proper adjective <u>twice</u>. Here's a sample to get you started:

<u>***Wild West***</u> **Pizza:** *Toppings include* <u>*sweet*</u> *onions;* <u>*hot*</u> *peppers; and chicken, beef, or sausage in a* <u>*spicy*</u> <u>*Texas*</u> *barbecue sauce.*

Composition Hint

Make your writing more concise by replacing a wordy expression with an adjective.

WORDY: The student researched several countries *that are on the continent of Asia*.

CONCISE: The student researched several *Asian* countries.
                                                          ADJ.

WORDY: Thank you for the offer *that shows generosity*.

CONCISE: Thank you for the *generous* offer.
                                        ADJ.

ACTIVITY 8

Rewrite each sentence, using an adjective instead of the italicized expression. The adjective may or may not be a proper adjective.

Samples:

a. The actor met with a producer *who works in Hollywood*.

   The actor met with a Hollywood producer.

b. Unfortunately, the remark *made without thinking* cost me a friendship.

   Unfortunately, the thoughtless remark cost me a friendship.

1. The seamstress relies on measurements *made with care*.

_____

2. Athletes *with great talent* must practice hard, nevertheless.

_____

3. Salmon *shipped in from Alaska* is today's special.

_____

4. San Francisco is known for its days *marked by fog*.

_____

5. Everyone appreciates friends *who show their support*.

_____

Another Composition Hint

Sometimes an adjective is redundant, or repeats what is already said in the sentence. Before using an adjective, make sure that it is needed.

QUESTION: Which word is unnecessary in the following sentence?

Cold, wet rain soaked through my shoes.

ANSWER: The adjective *wet* is not needed because all rain is wet. The sentence should read:

Cold rain soaked through my shoes.

ACTIVITY 9

Each sentence contains an adjective that is not needed. Write the redundant adjective on the line provided.

Sample:

The biker skinned his knee on the hard cement. _____hard_____

1. Our room had a view of tall, majestic mountains. _____

2. Each victorious winner will receive a trophy. _____

3. Would somebody explain the true facts to me? _____

4. Drizzle the cake with sweet, melted sugar. _____

5. A big boulder was blocking the mountain road. _____

Predicate Adjectives and Predicate Nouns

In some sentences, all we need to make a complete statement is a subject and a verb.

Sandy waved.
S.   V.

Snakes hiss.
S.   V.

But in other sentences, a subject and a verb may not be enough, especially if the verb is a linking verb.

Sandy *seems* . . .
S.   L.V.

Snakes *are* . . .
S.   L.V.

In each of the above two sentences, we must add a **complement** to the linking verb.

A *complement* is a word or expression that "completes" a sentence with a linking verb.

For example:

Sandy seems *friendly*.
    L.V.

(The adjective *friendly* is a complement of the linking verb *seems*.)

Snakes are *reptiles*.
    L.V.

(The noun *reptiles* is a complement of the linking verb *are*.)

ACTIVITY 10

Complete each sentence by writing a suitable complement after each italicized linking verb. Choose complements from the following list and use each one only once:

| difficult | mountains | scratchy | scientists | late | dark |
| enjoyable | res~~tl~~ess | nervous | planet | stale | |

> **Sample:**
>
> The audience became _____*restless*_____.

1. The Appalachians and the Rockies *are* _____.

2. This bread *tastes* _____.

3. By dinnertime, the day had *grown* _____.

4. Why *were* you _____?

5. Saturn *is* a _____.

6. That job interview *was* _____.

7. The homecoming dance *was* _____.

8. Newton and Einstein *were* _____.

9. Our graduation speaker *appeared* _____.

10. Does wool clothing always *feel* _____?

In the exercise you have just done, you used ten complements to complete ten linking verbs. You have been using complements all your life, even if you did not know they were called complements.

There are several kinds of complements. Here we study two of them:

1. the *predicate adjective*

2. the *predicate noun*

Together, predicate adjectives and predicate nouns are called *subject complements*.

We will now look more closely at the predicate adjective.

 A *predicate adjective* completes a linking verb and modifies the subject of that linking verb.

PREDICATE ADJECTIVES: The *sauce* smells *spicy*.
S.   L.V. PRED.ADJ.

(*Spicy* is a predicate adjective because it completes the linking verb *smells* and modifies the subject *sauce*.)

Percy was *honest*.
S.   L.V. PRED. ADJ.

(*Honest* is a predicate adjective because it completes the linking verb *was* and modifies the subject *Percy*.)

ACTIVITY 11

In each sentence, underline the linking verb. Then circle the predicate adjective and draw an arrow from it to the noun or pronoun it modifies.

Samples:

a. Your plans seem(ambitious.)

b. Has the field trip been(interesting?)

1. The day became windy.

2. People were suspicious.

3. Those icicles are beautiful.

4. Later, everyone seemed tired.

5. Rain forests are valuable.

6. After dark, the crickets sounded loud.

7. Lately, they have been attentive.

8. Was the concert good?

9. Your hair appears different today.

10. Do those crackers taste cheesy?

Predicate Nouns

 A *predicate noun* completes a linking verb and identifies or explains the subject of that linking verb.

Here is an example of a predicate noun.

The winner was a *sophomore*.
    S.   L.V.   PRED. N.

(*Sophomore* is a predicate noun because it completes the linking verb *was* and identifies the subject *winner*.)

Here are additional examples of predicate nouns.

Mark is a *journalist*.
  S. L.V.   PRED. N.

The tiny cub became a huge *bear*.
      S.   L.V.   PRED. N.

QUESTION: How can I find the predicate noun in a question?

ANSWER: Rewrite the question as a statement. The predicate noun is the noun that follows the linking verb.

QUESTION: Was your grandmother a teacher?

STATEMENT: Your grandmother *was* a *teacher*.

PREDICATE NOUN: *teacher*

ACTIVITY 12

In each sentence, underline the linking verb. Then circle the predicate noun and draw an arrow from it to the subject it identifies or explains.

> **Samples:**
>
> **a.** The intruder must have <u>been</u> a (raccoon.)
>
> **b.** <u>Was</u> Grover Cleveland a U.S. (president?)

1. Pluto is the smallest planet.

2. Your invitation was a surprise.

3. Were both women professional pilots?

4. Ginger Rogers became a famous dancer.

5. Are those trees redwoods?

6. Yes, Mei-Li is my older sister.

7. Our new kitten has been named Scooter.

8. Is Vincent's favorite class chemistry?

9. Was Hernando Cortés an explorer?

10. Walt Whitman has been called the first truly American poet.

Composition Hint

As writers, we often have a choice when we use a complement to explain or describe a subject. We can use either (1) a predicate noun or (2) a predicate adjective.

1. The thief was a *coward*.
   PRED. N.

   (The predicate noun *coward* identifies the subject *thief*.)

2. The thief was *cowardly*.
   PRED. ADJ.

   (The predicate adjective *cowardly* describes the subject *thief*.)

Become familiar with both choices. Then, when you write, you will be able to select the one that better expresses your idea in a particular situation.

ACTIVITY 13

Magda and four friends have formed a movie club. Each month, they view and discuss a movie together. In Magda's notes, shown below, she has used predicate nouns to explain or identify subjects. Help her revise her notes by replacing each predicate noun with a predicate adjective. Write your predicate adjective above the underlined predicate noun. One item is completed as a sample.

<u>My Movie Club Notes</u>

Movie: <u>Spider-Man</u>

           enjoyable
1. This movie was <u>an enjoyment</u> to watch.

2. Peter Parker is <u>a hero</u>.

3. His girlfriend is <u>a beauty</u>.

4. Certainly, the Green Goblin is <u>a spook</u>.

5. The soundtrack will be <u>a thrill</u> to music lovers.

6. Wow! The plot is <u>a real sensation</u>.

7. The main characters are <u>a wonder</u>.

8. Also, Spider-Man's powers are truly <u>a fantasy</u>.

9. Some special effects are <u>a shock</u>.

10. Peter and Mary Jane's kiss was <u>a delight</u>.

11. Overall, the movie was <u>a spectacle</u>.

Irvin is a member of Magda's movie club, described in Activity 13. Read the following page of Irvin's movie club notes. He has used predicate adjectives to modify subjects. Help him revise his notes by writing a predicate noun above each underlined predicate adjective. One item is completed as a sample.

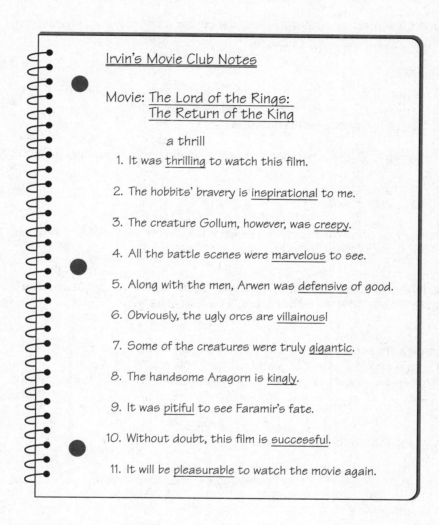

Irvin's Movie Club Notes

Movie: The Lord of the Rings:
The Return of the King

a thrill
1. It was thrilling to watch this film.

2. The hobbits' bravery is inspirational to me.

3. The creature Gollum, however, was creepy.

4. All the battle scenes were marvelous to see.

5. Along with the men, Arwen was defensive of good.

6. Obviously, the ugly orcs are villainous!

7. Some of the creatures were truly gigantic.

8. The handsome Aragorn is kingly.

9. It was pitiful to see Faramir's fate.

10. Without doubt, this film is successful.

11. It will be pleasurable to watch the movie again.

Writing
Application

Using Predicate Adjectives
and Predicate Nouns

Choose a movie, a CD, or a book to review. Using the movie club reviews as a model (see Activities 13 and 14), write **ten** statements or judgments about the item you are reviewing. In each statement, use a predicate adjective or a predicate noun. Then underline and label each predicate adjective or predicate noun.

10 Adverbs

Suppose you glance at the headlines in today's newspaper and read the following:

"Fire Blazes!"

After reading this short statement, you probably want to know the answers to certain questions:

1. *How* or *to what extent* did the fire blaze?

2. *When* did it blaze?

3. *Where* did it blaze?

Words that tell *how, when,* or *where* are **adverbs**.

If the reporter answers the above questions by using adverbs, the first sentence in the article may read like this:

"A fire blazed *wildly today downtown.*"

With these details, you know *how* the fire blazed *(wildly)*, *when* it blazed *(today)*, and *where* it blazed *(downtown)*. Adverbs make the difference.

 An *adverb* is a word that modifies (1) a verb, (2) an adjective, or (3) another adverb. Adverbs tell *how, to what extent, when,* or *where.*

Many adverbs end in *ly,* such as *wildly, quickly* and *suddenly*. Other words that can be used as adverbs do not end in *ly,* such as *today, fast,* and *behind.*

We will look at the three uses of adverbs one at a time. First, let's look at how adverbs modify verbs.

(1) An adverb is a word that modifies a verb.

We *eat daily*.
    v. ADV.

(The adverb *daily* modifies the verb *eat* and tells *when*.)

Ricardo *walked downtown*.
      v.   ADV.

(The adverb *downtown* modifies the verb *walked* and tells *where*.)

Carol *did not understand*.
    v. ADV.

(The adverb *not* modifies the verb *did understand* and tells *how*.)

In each sentence, underline the adverb. Then draw an arrow from the adverb to the verb it modifies.

> **Samples:**
>
> **a.** Paulo caught the ball <u>easily</u>.
>
> **b.** I do <u>not</u> remember your name.

1. The ballerina danced <u>gracefully</u>.

2. Your science textbook is <u>there</u>.

3. This software does <u>not</u> work.

4. My teammates cheered <u>happily</u>.

5. Nora sketched <u>carelessly</u> on the book cover.

QUESTION: Where does the adverb go in the sentence?

ANSWER: Often, an adverb may come before or after a verb in a sentence.

Occasionally Mr. Cheski *coughed*.

Mr. Cheski *occasionally* *coughed*.

Mr. Cheski *coughed* *occasionally*.

ESL Focus

Placement of Adverbs

Do not put an adverb between a verb and its object. In the following example, *items* is the direct object of the verb *stacked*. The adverb *carefully* must not come between the verb and the object.

> The shopkeeper *stacked* items *carefully*.
>   VERB   OBJECT

Advarb

> The shopkeeper *carefully* stacked items.
>   VERB   OBJECT

> (NOT *The shopkeeper stacked carefully items*.)

Here is another example.

> Tino *sometimes* cooks meat.
>   VERB OBJECT

> Tino cooks meat *sometimes*.
>   VERB OBJECT

> (NOT *Tino cooks sometimes meat*.)

QUESTION: Can more than one adverb modify the same verb?

ANSWER: Yes, two or more adverbs may modify the same verb.

Onstage, the ballerina danced _gracefully_. (Both adverbs modify _danced_.)

Finally Jarrell fell _tiredly_ into bed. (Both adverbs modify _fell_.)

ACTIVITY 2

Underline each adverb. Then draw an arrow from the adverb to the verb it modifies. Some sentences have more than one adverb.

Samples:

a. Tomorrow we will finish this lesson.

b. Erin always completes assignments neatly.

1. The skies finally cleared.

2. Patiently, Naomi waited for Robbie.

3. The student driver slowly and intently parked.

4. Unfortunately, the seeds did not sprout.

5. Sometimes you really annoy me.

6. The officers certainly deserve our gratitude.

7. The subway always runs reliably.

8. I often dream vividly during the night.

9. Suddenly a bug bit my arm.

10. Water trickled musically downstream.

(2) An adverb is a word that modifies an adjective.

Mom served _extremely_ sweet tea.
ADV. ADJ.

(The adverb _extremely_ modifies the adjective _sweet_ and tells _how_ sweet.)

The children were _charmingly_ polite.
ADV. ADJ.

(The adverb _charmingly_ modifies the adjective _polite_ and tells _to what extent_.)

That is a _very_ nasty cut.
ADV. ADJ.

(The adverb _very_ modifies the adjective _nasty_ and tells _how_ nasty.)

Placement of Adverbs

When an adverb modifies an adjective, it always comes before the adjective.

The line was _perfectly straight_.

(NOT _The line was straight perfectly._)

ACTIVITY 3 _____

Underline each adverb. Then, draw an arrow from the adverb to the adjective it modifies.

Samples:

a. This <u>surprisingly</u> tasty bread is homemade.

b. In the sky hovered a <u>perfectly</u> round object.

1. Your volunteer work is <u>certainly</u> admirable.

2. A <u>very</u> expensive necklace was stolen.

3. Are the shoes <u>too</u> tight?

4. My <u>annoyingly</u> perfect brother won first place.

5. Ms. Romero is <u>consistently</u> punctual.

6. Latasha's temperament is <u>naturally</u> cheerful.

7. The Tornadoes' goalie has become <u>quite</u> skillful.

8. I am <u>genuinely</u> regretful about the mistake.

9. The <u>unusually</u> difficult midterm took an hour.

10. Milo's ideas were <u>always</u> wacky.

(3) An adverb is a word that modifies another adverb.

You gave up _too easily_.
    ADV. ADV.

(The adverb _too_ modifies the adverb _easily_ and tells _how_ easily.)

Jordan jogs _fairly regularly_.
    ADV.   ADV.

(The adverb _fairly_ modifies the adverb _regularly_ and tells _how_ regularly.)

Rosie _very politely_ refused.
  ADV. ADV.

(The adverb _very_ modifies the adverb _politely_ and tells _to what extent_.)

ACTIVITY 4

Underline the two adverbs in each sentence. Then draw an arrow from each adverb to the word it modifies.

Sample:

That is <u>not</u> <u>entirely</u> true.

1. The tiger snarled <u>rather</u> <u>frightfully</u>.

2. Skyler is <u>almost</u> <u>always</u> pleasant.

3. <u>Much</u> <u>earlier</u>, the bridge had collapsed.

4. Ramona speaks German <u>nearly</u> <u>flawlessly</u>.

5. Think <u>very</u> <u>carefully</u> about each test question.

SUMMARY: An adverb is a word that modifies (1) a verb, (2) an adjective, or (3) another adverb.

ACTIVITY 5

For each sentence, explain why the italicized word is an adverb. You may use these abbreviations:

verb (v.)   adjective (adj.)   adverb (adv.)

Sample:

Soon the race will begin. _____*Soon*_____ modifies the __*v. will begin*__.

1. Sausage sizzled *quietly*. _____ modifies the _____.

2. The *too* bright light blinded me. _____ modifies the _____.

3. *Certainly,* we will support you. _____ modifies the _____.

4. He *just* barely caught the bus. _____ modifies the _____.

5. Thriftiness is *indeed* admirable. _____ modifies the _____.

6. I *rather* boldly took the last slice. _____ modifies the _____.

7. Tariq waved *casually* at Philip. _____ modifies the _____.

8. Our kiss was *so* sweet! _____ modifies the _____.

9. Pam *eagerly* grabbed the money. _____ modifies the _____.

10. She *very* quickly agreed. _____ modifies the _____.

Using Adverbs

On a separate sheet of paper, write **ten** sentences about what you did last weekend. Use an adverb in three of the sentences but not in the other seven. Then, with your teacher's approval, exchange sentences with a classmate.

Rewrite all ten of your classmate's sentences, making them more clear and vivid by adding at least one adverb to each one. (In each of the three sentences that already have adverbs, add an adverb to modify the existing adverb.) Finally, underline each adverb and draw an arrow from it to the verb, adjective, or adverb it modifies. Share the results with your classmate.

Forming Adverbs from Adjectives

To form adverbs from adjectives, follow these guidelines.

I. Most adverbs are formed by adding *ly* to an adjective.

ADJECTIVE		ADVERB
careful	+ ly =	carefully
pure	+ ly =	purely

II. If an adjective ends in *ic*, add *al* before adding *ly*.

ADJECTIVE		ADVERB
basic	+ ly =	basically
specific	+ ly =	specifically

III. If an adjective ends in *y*, change the *y* to *i* and then add *ly*.

ADJECTIVE				ADVERB
merry	⟶	(merri)	+ ly =	merrily
funny	⟶	(funni)	+ ly =	funnily

IV. If an adjective ends in *le*, do not add *ly*; simply change *le* to *ly*.

ADJECTIVE		ADVERB
gentle	⟶	gently
terrible	⟶	terribly

ACTIVITY 6

Follow the directions below to fill in the puzzle.

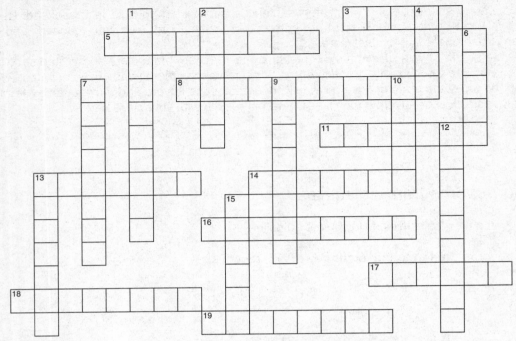

ACROSS: Adverbs

Change each adjective to an adverb. Use the adverbs to fill in the puzzle.

Samples:

ADJECTIVE	ADVERB
crazy	*crazily*
agreeable	*agreeably*

3. true _____

5. amazing _____

8. graphic _____

11. quick _____

13. shaky _____

14. final _____

16. foolish _____

17. snug _____

18. suitable _____

19. mental _____

DOWN: Adjectives

Change each adverb to an adjective. Use the adjectives to fill in the puzzle.

Samples:

ADVERB	ADJECTIVE
merrily	*merry*
patiently	*patient*

1. impressively _____

2. fiercely _____

4. lazily _____

6. noisily _____

7. adorably _____

9. horribly _____

10. luckily _____

12. lethargically _____

13. seriously _____

15. hoarsely _____

Composition Hint

Adverbs can help us express ourselves more concisely. Compare the following examples.

WORDY: The team practiced *in an energetic manner*.

CONCISE: The team practiced *energetically*.

ACTIVITY 7

In each sentence, what adverb can you use to express the italicized thought concisely? Write the adverb on the line provided.

Samples:

a. The firefighter worked *like a heroic person*.   heroically

b. The herd moved *at a rapid pace*.   rapidly

1. Kirk gobbled his sandwich *in a hungry fashion*.   _____

2. Gigi yelled *with a furious attitude* at Lola.   _____

3. Is the trailer hooked *in a secure way* to the truck?   _____

4. The clerk stared at me *with a strange look*.   _____

5. I couldn't help but laugh *in a hysterical manner*.   _____

6. Let's solve the problem *using creative means*.   _____

7. Jo always dresses *in a fashionable style*.   _____

8. *Under usual circumstances*, I would ride the bus.   _____

9. Please explain the process *with precise language*.   _____

10. Doug answered me *from an honest perspective*.   _____

Recognizing Adverbs and Adjectives

Most words that end in *ly* are adverbs, *but not all of them*. To tell whether or not a particular word is an adverb, look at how the word is used in the sentence.

ADJECTIVE: Paige earns a *weekly* paycheck.

(The adjective *weekly* modifies the noun *paycheck*.)

ADVERB: Paige is paid *weekly*.

(The adverb *weekly* modifies the verb *is paid*.)

Likewise, some words that do not end in *ly* can be adverbs or adjectives. To decide the word's part of speech, look at how it is used in the sentence.

ADJECTIVE: Paige's job is *hard*.

(The adjective *hard* modifies the noun *job*.)

ADVERB: Paige works *hard*.

(The adverb *hard* modifies the verb *works*.)

ACTIVITY 8

Draw an arrow from each italicized word to the word it modifies. If the italicized word is used as an adjective, write *adj.* on the line provided. If it is used as an adverb, write *adv*.

> **Samples:**
>
> __adv.__ **a.** The dart fell *short* of the dartboard.
>
> __adj.__ **b.** Sporty, *fast* cars fascinate me.

_____ **1.** Is your dog *friendly?*

_____ **2.** Sonny's speech was *well* done.

_____ **3.** Alison's hair becomes *curly* in the rain.

_____ **4.** The lawyer's *hourly* rate seems fair.

_____ **5.** Ripe fruit hung *low* on the branches.

_____ **6.** Think of the solution *fast!*

_____ **7.** Justina cleans the closets *yearly*.

_____ **8.** Several *long* banners announced a dance.

_____ **9.** This morning, happy birds sang *early*.

_____ **10.** Was the judge's decision *just?*

SUMMARY: Do not automatically assume a word is or is not an adverb because of an ending in *ly*. Instead, look at how the word is used in the sentence and then decide the word's part of speech.

11 Review of Adjectives and Adverbs

An **adjective** is a word that modifies a noun or pronoun. An **adverb** is a word that modifies a verb, an adjective, or another adverb. To decide whether a word is an adjective or an adverb, look at how it is used in the sentence.

ACTIVITY 1

Underline the correct choice in each pair of italicized words. On the line provided, write whether the word is used as an adjective (adj.) or adverb (adv.).

> **Samples:**
>
> ___adj.___ **a.** Kasey is a plain and (<u>practical</u>, practically) person.
>
> ___adv.___ **b.** In his panic, Julio (practical, <u>practically</u>) shouted at me.

_____ **1.** We (proud, proudly) Panthers will trounce the Tigers!

_____ **2.** Ms. Parker (proud, proudly) displayed several students' drawings.

_____ **3.** Whoops! I (near, nearly) missed the turnoff.

_____ **4.** Whew! That was a (near, nearly) escape!

_____ **5.** That girl talks on the telephone (hour, hourly).

_____ **6.** As a security guard, Ricky made (hour, hourly) rounds of the building.

_____ **7.** An outer space theme is the committee's (probable, probably) choice.

_____ **8.** You are (probable, probably) not late yet.

_____ **9.** I have prepared a (brief, briefly) presentation.

_____ **10.** (Brief, Briefly), the umpire consulted a clipboard.

_____ **11.** The engine is (real, really) quite powerful!

_____ **12.** A (real, really) counterfeit bill may be difficult to spot.

_____ **13.** Do you have a (clear, clearly) view?

_____ **14.** (Clear, Clearly), they should have asked permission first.

_____ **15.** A storm blew in (sudden, suddenly).

_____ **16.** Your decision to leave was certainly (sudden, suddenly).

_____ **17.** The gold ring was (impossible, impossibly) tiny.

_____ **18.** An (*impossible, impossibly*) task lay before the captain.

_____ **19.** The wind (*rare, rarely*) blows here.

_____ **20.** His measurements are (*rare, rarely*) accurate.

For Activities 2 and 3, read the following passage.

The Mermaid's Man

Lazily, the mermaid swished her silver tail. Carelessly, she pushed silky hair from her eyes. With an upward gaze, she watched the water's surface. The dark shape of a boat appeared overhead, and she softly sighed. The boat passed nightly, and she knew it held a young man who went to meet his beloved. Oh, the mermaid envied this woman! If a man would love her so ardently . . . well, she could be truly content forever.

The mermaid twirled her hair and gave the idea some thought. *Her own man.* With a sly smile, she swished her tail and swam straight upward. With one hand she pushed against the boat's edge. It tilted slowly, slowly, until its human cargo fell into the sea. The man splashed and gasped, but eventually he sank. The mermaid was there to embrace him and to take him into her underwater cave. *Her very own man!*

ACTIVITY 2 _____

The passage contains 25 adjectives. On the lines below, write each adjective and the noun it modifies. Do not include the articles *a, an,* and *the*. The first item is completed as a sample.

	ADJECTIVE	NOUN
1.	her	tail
2.		
3.		
4.		
5.		
6.		
7.		
8.		
9.		
10.		
11.		

12. _____   _____

13. _____   _____

14. _____   _____

15. _____   _____

16. _____   _____

17. _____   _____

18. _____   _____

19. _____   _____

20. _____   _____

21. _____   _____

22. _____   _____

23. _____   _____

24. _____   _____

25. _____   _____

ACTIVITY 3

The passage contains 16 adverbs. Below, list each adverb and the word it modifies, including the word's part of speech (*v.* for *verb, adj.* for *adjective, adv.* for *adverb*). The first item is completed as a sample.

ADVERB	WORD MODIFIED
1. Lazily	swished
2.	
3.	
4.	
5.	
6.	
7.	
8.	
9.	
10.	

11. _____   _____

12. _____   _____

13. _____   _____

14. _____   _____

15. _____   _____

16. _____   _____

 Writing
Application

Using Adjectives and Adverbs

In "The Mermaid's Man," what do you think happens next? On a separate sheet of paper, write **two** paragraphs of at least **five** sentences each, continuing the tale. Your story can be funny, romantic, poetic, action-packed—it's up to you. Use at least **five adjectives** and **five adverbs** in your story. Underline and label each one.

ACTIVITY 4 _____

Sort the words in bold type into two lists: adjectives and adverbs. Then fit the words into the appropriate puzzle forward, backward, up, or down. The words in each puzzle interlock.

rusty wagon   behaving **badly**

sadly crying   **small** feet

run **far** away   **barely** visible

safe activity   arrived **safely**

loud voice   **sneaky** boy

ADJECTIVES   ADVERBS

_____   _____

_____   _____

_____   _____

_____   _____

Adjectives   Adverbs

For Activities 5 and 6, read the following poem.

Meeting at Night
Robert Browning

The grey sea and the long black land;

And the yellow half-moon large and low;

And the startled little waves that leap

In fiery ringlets from their sleep,

As I gain the cove with pushing prow,

And quench its speed i' the slushy sand.

Then a mile of warm sea-scented beach;

Three fields to cross till a farm appears;

A tap at the pane, the quick sharp scratch

And blue spurt of a lighted match,

And a voice less loud, thro' its joys and fears,

Than the two hearts beating each to each!

ACTIVITY 5

To create vivid, precise ideas, Browning uses at least one adjective in each line of the poem. Choose two ideas that are expressed using adjectives in the poem. On the lines below, write the phrase or line(s) that express each idea and circle the adjective(s). Then explain why the idea appeals to you.

> **Sample:**
>
> *a. phrase or lines:*   "a mile of (warm) (sea-scented) beach"
>
> *b. why you like the idea:*   These adjectives appeal to my senses of touch and
>
> smell. The image makes me think of warm, gritty sand between my bare toes,
>
> and the smell of salt air that clings to my hair after a trip to the beach.

1. *a. phrase or lines:* _____

   b. why you like the idea: _____

   _____

   _____

   _____

2. *a. phrase or lines:* _____

   b. why you like the idea: _____

_____

_____

_____

_____

ACTIVITY 6 _____

Refer to "Meeting at Night" to complete each item.

1. In the entire poem, Browning uses only one adverb. What is this adverb? _____

2. Why do you think Browning uses only one adverb but many adjectives in this poem?

_____

_____

_____

_____

_____

Writing
Application

Using Adjectives and Adverbs

What do you think is happening in Browning's poem "Meeting at Night"? Exactly who is meeting, and why, and why at night?

On a separate sheet of paper, write **two** paragraphs of at least **five** sentences each explaining your interpretation of the poem. Using Browning as inspiration, choose creative—even poetic—adjectives and adverbs to use in your description. (A thesaurus may come in handy.) Underline and label each adjective and adverb in your response.

12 Prepositions

A *preposition* relates a noun or pronoun to some other part of the sentence.

Here are some examples of prepositions in sentences.

1. The softball *rolled under* a *bush*.
　　　　　　　V.　PREP.　　N.

(The preposition *under* relates the noun *bush* to the verb *rolled*.)

2. *Snacks for everyone* are available.
　　　N.　PREP.　PRON.

(The preposition *for* relates the pronoun *everyone* to the noun *Snacks*.)

3. We are *happy about* the *score*.
　　　　　　ADJ.　PREP.　　N.

(The preposition *about* relates the noun *score* to the adjective *happy*.)

4. Dan drove *quickly despite* the *rain*.
　　　　　　ADV.　PREP.　　N.

(The preposition *despite* relates the noun *rain* to the adverb *quickly*.)

Common Prepositions

Here is a list of words commonly used as prepositions. Notice that some prepositions, such as *in spite of*, are made up of more than one word. In the chart below, blank spaces are provided for you to fill in additional prepositions from the puzzle in Activity 1.

about	_____	in front of	_____
_____	beneath	_____	throughout
across	beside	in spite of	till
after	_____	instead of	to
_____	beyond	_____	_____
along	but (meaning "except")	like	under
alongside	by	of	_____
among	despite	_____	up
around	_____	on	upon
as	during	out of	with
at	except	_____	_____
because of	for	_____	without
before	_____	past	
behind	in	since	

ACTIVITY 1

Fifteen one-word prepositions are hidden in this puzzle. Each has three or more letters. They may be embedded forward, backward, up, down, and diagonally. Find and circle the fifteen prepositions on your own or, with your teacher's approval, work with a classmate. Write each one in alphabetical order to complete the list of Common Prepositions on page 107.

```
A I W Y F W I T H I N Q
I B O E P R L A X E C E
L Q L E W K R M O R F I
H H E D I S T U O D N U
G A B M Z D F H C T K M
U J Q Y R X V F O V E R
O F F A P J A E W R G N
R E W U H C D S A A L N
H O A G A I N S T B V E
T Z G W S M U K H O S E
U S V N D Q J N Z V I W
R K I J O V D F T E U T
O U Q D W F M R S I O E
C O H E N X L V D B L B
```

ACTIVITY 2

Complete each sentence by writing a preposition on the blank.

Sample:

Snow has been falling ___*since*___ Tuesday.

1. Everyone _____ Sandra rides the bus to school.

2. _____ my bed are socks, candy wrappers, and dust balls.

3. My best friend is happy _____ our weekend plans.

4. You'll get soaked immediately _____ an umbrella.

5. The caterpillar breathes _____ holes called spiracles.

6. _____ dinnertime, I must babysit my little brother.

7. Georgia has started eating salads _____ French fries.

8. This old letter is faded _____ the edges.

9. Those _____ permission slips may board the bus.

10. The fruit bat sucks juice _____ fruit.

Some words that are used as prepositions may also be used as adverbs.

PREPOSITION: Principal Jensen waited *outside* the classroom.

(The preposition *outside* relates the noun *classroom* to the verb *waited*.)

ADVERB: Principal Jensen waited *outside*.

(The adverb *outside* modifies the verb *waited*.)

QUESTION: How can I tell whether a word is used as a preposition or an adverb?

ANSWER: Look at how the word is used in the sentence, and remember these two facts:

• A preposition *always* relates a noun or pronoun to another part of the sentence. Look for that noun or pronoun to confirm the word's use as a preposition.

• An adverb *never* relates a noun or pronoun to another part of the sentence. Instead, it modifies a verb, an adjective, or an adverb.

Be sure to look at how a word is used in a sentence before deciding whether it is a preposition or an adverb.

ACTIVITY 3

If the italicized word is used as a preposition, write *prep.* on the line provided. If the word is used as an adverb, write *adv.*

Samples:

prep **a.** *Beneath* the sofa, Garrett found a twenty-dollar bill.

adv. **b.** Ginger walked *past* without a word.

_____ **1.** Janice accidentally left her wallet *behind*.

_____ **2.** Leave those muddy boots *outside* the house.

_____ **3.** The cow jumped *over* the moon.

_____ **4.** Have you read poems by John Keats *before*?

_____ **5.** *Before* the blackboard stood our new geometry teacher.

_____ **6.** Put that crystal figurine *down,* please.

_____ **7.** A green worm inched *toward* a tasty leaf.

_____ **8.** *Below* the surface, a dolphin swam.

_____ **9.** Oh, bother. I am locked *out*.

_____ **10.** Dark clouds scudded *past* the full moon.

Object of the Preposition

You have probably noticed by now that every preposition is followed by a noun or a pronoun.

The Nguyen family lives *across town*.
                 PREP.

The noun or pronoun that follows a preposition is the *object of the preposition*.

The Nguyen family lives *across* *town*.
　　　　　　　　　　　　　PREP.　OBJ. OF PREP.

I'll make an exception *for* *you*.
　　　　　　　　　　PREP. OBJ. OF PREP.

ACTIVITY 4 _____

For each sentence, underline the preposition <u>once</u> and underline the object of the preposition <u>twice</u>.

> **Samples:**
>
> **a.** <u>In spite of</u> the <u>heat</u>, Coach Fellows told us to run laps.
>
> **b.** Fool's gold sparkled <u>among</u> the <u>rocks</u>.

1. Oh! My new earring fell down the drain.

2. Because of him, I enjoy chess club.

3. Everyone's talking about your performance.

4. Throughout the store, shoppers examined merchandise.

5. Meet me outside the mall.

6. Mr. Farris planted red pansies along the walk.

7. For a moment, no one said a word.

8. Heather wanted tomato soup instead of a sandwich.

9. Between these bookends are my textbooks.

10. Who dumped the breakfast cereal out of the box?

Prepositional Phrases

As you know, a preposition relates a noun or pronoun (its object) to another word in the sentence.

A comet streaked *across* the *sky*.
　　　　　　　　　　PREP.　　　OBJ. OF PREP.

(The preposition *across* relates the noun *sky* to the verb *streaked*.)

Together, the preposition and its object make up a *prepositional phrase*.

A *prepositional phrase* is a group of words that (1) begins with a *preposition* and (2) ends with the *object of the preposition* (a noun or pronoun).

A comet streaked *across the sky.*
PREP. PHRASE

Near her was an artist's portfolio.
PREP. PHRASE

A word that modifies the object of the preposition is considered part of the prepositional phrase.

A comet streaked *across the starry sky.*
PREP. PHRASE

A comet streaked *across the dark and starry sky.*
PREP. PHRASE

Gabe read every article *inside the sports magazine.*
PREP. PHRASE

ACTIVITY 5

Underline each prepositional phrase in the following passage. There are 16 prepositional phrases, including the one underlined as a sample. Some sentences do not have a prepositional phrase.

Tch! Tch! Tch! Something was scratching at the back door. What was outdoors in the dark making that spooky noise? Did it have big teeth in a hungry mouth? Why couldn't my first night alone overnight be uneventful? Now I wished Aunt Polly or even Grandma were staying with me. Either one of them would march boldly <u>to the back door</u>. She would peer through the curtains. With a chuckle, she would say, "Just a raccoon. Told you so."

"Well," I said aloud to myself, "If you can't *be* brave, then *act* brave." I grabbed a stainless steel pot from the cabinet. I grabbed a long metal spoon, too, and rushed at the back door. I banged the spoon on the pot as loudly as possible. At the same time, I yelled, "Aaaaaaahhhhhhhh!" I sounded like a Viking warrior.

I heard a startled yelp outside. The canine voice sounded familiar. Then something occurred to me. The family dog, Spritzy, was in the backyard.

 Writing Application

Using Prepositional Phrases

Have you ever been afraid of something that turned out to be nonthreatening after all? Maybe it was a person, an event such as your first date, or an activity such as staying home alone overnight.

On a separate sheet of paper, write **two** paragraphs of at least **five** sentences each, telling about the experience, explaining what seemed frightening, and telling how you realized is was not scary after all. Underline each prepositional phrase in your paragraphs.

QUESTION: Can a preposition have more than one object?

ANSWER: Yes, a preposition can have more than one object. Two or more objects of the same preposition are called a *compound object.*

Please draw a map *for <u>Kris</u> and <u>me</u>.* (two objects of the preposition *for*)
COMPOUND OBJ.

Please draw a map *for <u>Kris</u>, <u>Reggie</u>, and <u>me</u>.* (three objects of the preposition *for*)
COMPOUND OBJ.

QUESTION: Can a sentence have more than one prepositional phrase?

ANSWER: Yes, a sentence can have as many prepositional phrases as it needs.

A package *for you* came *in today's mail.*

A package *for you from Terrell* came *in today's mail.*

ACTIVITY 6

Underline each prepositional phrase in the following sentences. If the preposition has more than one object, be sure to underline the entire compound object.

> **Samples:**
>
> **a.** Hector wants to buy the surfboard <u>in the corner</u> <u>of the display case</u>.
>
> **b.** I need money <u>for a ball, bat, and glove</u>.

1. During her turn at bat, DeeDee hit a home run.

2. On rainy days, the class plays dodgeball in the gym.

3. The hot dog vendor got business from teachers, students, and parents.

4. Kick the ball past the goalie and into the net.

5. Mike and I will play tennis doubles with you and Wilson.

6. The bus for the coach and volleyball players will arrive shortly.

7. The basketball players in orange jerseys are from my school.

8. Over the loudspeakers, Coach Frank reported on the game in a loud voice.

9. I cannot play without my lucky key chain in my pocket.

10. Shelby is on the track team with Claudette, Suzette, and Nanette.

Composition Hint

Prepositional phrases help make our writing more clear and specific by providing important details. Consider the following sentence, written without a prepositional phrase.

> A black widow spider is hiding.

Now look at the sentence, revised to include a prepositional phrase.

> A black widow spider is hiding *behind that door*.

ACTIVITY 7

Rewrite each sentence, making its meaning more precise by adding one or more prepositional phrases.

Samples:

a. Bridget dropped the glass.

Bridget dropped the glass into soapy dishwater.

b. The one is mine.

The one near the test tubes on the lab table is mine.

1. The box is ready.

2. Please take this.

3. Josie crossed the finish line.

4. Your friends are waiting.

5. Why don't you wear the sweater?

6. The joints are wobbly.

7. I'll wait.

8. Please help Professor Platt look.

9. The campus newspaper needs articles.

_____

10. Corey is saving his money.

_____

 Writing
Application

Using Prepositional Phrases
for Precise Meaning

Using the sentences in Activity 7 as examples, write **five** sentences **without** prepositional phrases. Write on a separate sheet of paper. Then, with your teacher's approval, exchange sentences with a classmate. Rewrite each of your classmate's sentences, making them more precise by adding prepositional phrases. Share the results with your classmate.

Another Composition Hint

In casual conversation, we sometimes end a sentence with a preposition.

Theft is what I was afraid _of_.

Ending a sentence with a preposition separates the preposition from its object. It also makes a sentence wordy. Therefore, try to avoid ending a sentence with a preposition, especially in formal writing for school and work.

INSTEAD OF: Theft is what I was afraid _of_.

WRITE: I was afraid _of theft_.

ACTIVITY 8

Rewrite each sentence so that it does not end in a preposition.

> **Samples:**
>
> **a.** Whom did you speak to?
>
> _To whom did you speak?_
>
> **b.** Where are these ants coming from?
>
> _From where are these ants coming?_

1. Yes, the earthquake is what we were talking about.

_____

2. A ship is something I've never been on.

_____

3. What did you put the leftovers in?

_____

4. That rock is what I tripped over.

_____

5. Whom are you making the card for?

_____

13 Conjunctions

> A *conjunction* connects other words or groups of words.

Commonly used conjunctions include *and, but, or, nor, for* and *yet.* These particular conjunctions are the **coordinating conjunctions**.

What Kinds of Work Do Conjunctions Do?

1. **A conjunction connects *nouns*.**

    Scissors and glue are in the cabinet.

    Glue, paste, or tape will do the job.

2. **A conjunction connects *adjectives*.**

    Strange but fascinating artwork covered the walls.

    His sketches are *simple, small, and funny*.

3. **A conjunction connects *verbs*.**

    Our art teacher *cut and folded* the paper.

    I *will borrow or buy* some charcoal.

4. **A conjunction connects *pronouns* or *nouns and pronouns*.**

    You and he will share supplies.

    Borrow paint from *Gus, Olivia, or me*.

5. **A conjunction connects *adverbs*.**

    Shane shaped the clay *quickly yet carefully*.

    Slowly but surely, the tortoise won the race.

6. **A conjunction connects *prepositional phrases*.**

    Students worked *at desks, on the floor, and at easels*.

    On the ground and in the air, our flight team has your safety at heart.

In addition to the examples above, conjunctions can make still other connections, as we shall see later in the lesson.

Circle the conjunction in each sentence. Then underline each element it connects.

> **Samples:**
>
> **a.** The paintbrushes are <u>in the top drawer</u> (or) <u>on the counter</u>.
>
> **b.** <u>Slowly</u>, <u>steadily</u>, (and) <u>impressively</u>, the art show took shape.

1. Can you paint, draw, or sculpt?

2. Jordan's collage contained buttons, fabric, and beads.

3. Steadily and accurately, Luis sketched a helicopter.

4. The teacher said my still-life paintings are adequate but unoriginal.

5. You can soften the charcoal lines with a finger or with an eraser.

6. Bailey, Ashlee, or I will clean up our area.

7. These splashes of color are bold yet harmonious.

8. In the park, beside the lake, or beneath a tree is where I work best.

9. I sing, dance, and act—through my artwork.

10. For me, drawing human faces is difficult but rewarding.

Composition Hint

Conjunctions join words or word groups of *equal rank*, such as two nouns, two verbs, or two phrases.

POOR: Family rules can be *reassuring* yet a *frustration*.

(The words connected are not of equal rank. *Reassuring* is an adjective, but *frustration* is a noun.)

BETTER: Family rules can be *reassuring* yet *frustrating*.

(The words connected are of equal rank: They are both adjectives.)

Connecting similar elements creates a balance, called **parallel structure**, in your sentence. Nouns are similar, or *parallel* to, nouns and pronouns. Verbs are parallel to verbs, adjectives to adjectives, and so on.

Circle the conjunction in each sentence. If the conjunction joins elements of equal rank, write *correct* on the line provided. If the elements are not equal, rewrite the sentence using equal elements.

Samples:

a. After school, I must mow the lawn (and) other work.

 After school, I must mow the lawn and do other work.

b. The procedure was quick (and) painless.

 correct

1. To interest me, a book must be short and with humor.

_____

2. The hermit crab moved slowly yet with steadiness.

_____

3. The toast with jam but without butter is mine.

_____

4. LeeAnn made Valentines for Lily, Bobbie, and for me.

_____

5. I felt pleased and pride.

_____

6. *Maniac Magee* was written with humor and cleverly.

_____

7. Coral reefs thrive in water that is warm, clean, and salty.

_____

8. Jamal's decision to break up was a difficulty but necessary.

_____

9. Was the quiz a challenge or easy?

_____

10. Reginald quickly and with ease solved the math problem.

_____

Combining Simple Sentences

Another use for conjunctions is to combine *simple sentences* into *compound sentences*. For this purpose, the most commonly used conjunctions are *and, but,* and *or.*

 A *simple sentence* has only one subject and one verb.

SIMPLE SENTENCES: *Gilbert* always *plays* first base. *I* usually *pitch*.
                                   S.   V.   S.   V.

This *flight is* full. Another *one will be* available soon.
          S.   V.   S.   V.

 A *compound sentence* consists of two or more simple sentences, usually joined by a conjunction.

COMPOUND SENTENCES: Gilbert always plays first base, *and* I usually pitch.
                                          SIMPLE SENTENCE   CONJ. SIMPLE SENTENCE

This flight is full, *but* another one will be available soon.
SIMPLE SENTENCE   CONJ.   SIMPLE SENTENCE

ACTIVITY 3

Underline each subject <u>once</u> and each verb <u>twice</u>. If there is a conjunction, circle it. Then, if the sentence is *simple*, write S on the line provided. If it is *compound*, write C on the line. *(Hint: The subject of a sentence is never in a prepositional phrase.)*

> **Samples:**
>
> __*S*__ **a.** Zeus <u>ranked</u> highest among the Greek gods.
>
> __*C*__ **b.** Poseidon <u>was</u> his brother, (and) Hestia <u>was</u> his sister.

_____ **1.** Poseidon ruled the sea, but Hades ruled the underworld.

_____ **2.** Hades was also a brother to Zeus.

_____ **3.** Artemis was Zeus's daughter, and her twin brother was Apollo.

_____ **4.** One of my favorites is Aphrodite, goddess of love.

_____ **5.** The Romans knew her as Venus.

_____ **6.** We can use Greek names for the gods, or we can use Roman names.

_____ **7.** The Roman name for Zeus was Jupiter.

_____ **8.** The Greeks called the god of war Ares, but Romans called him Mars.

_____ **9.** I read Greek myths in books, or I read them on the Internet.

_____ **10.** Some planets in our solar system have the names of Roman gods.

QUESTION: Does a compound sentence need any special punctuation?

ANSWER: Yes, a comma [,] usually precedes the conjunction in a compound sentence.

The fire alarm sounded, *but* it was just a drill.

QUESTION: Does it matter which conjunction I use to join simple sentences?

ANSWER: Yes, it matters. Different conjunctions have different purposes, as explained below.

1. Use the conjunction *and* to join sentences that express equal thoughts.

EXAMPLE: A wooden *arm came* down. The *train rushed* by. (*simple sentences*)
          S.   V.   S.   V.

A wooden arm came down, *and* the train rushed by. (compound sentence)
    SIMPLE SENTENCE   CONJ. SIMPLE SENTENCE

2. Use the conjunction *but* to join sentences that contrast with each other.

EXAMPLE: *I got* new eyeglasses. *Nobody noticed* them. (*simple sentences*)
          S. V.   S.   V.

I got new eyeglasses, *but* nobody noticed them. (*compound sentence*)
    SIMPLE SENTENCE   CONJ. SIMPLE SENTENCE

3. Use the conjunction *or* to join sentences that express two or more possibilities.

EXAMPLE: *We could eat* healthfully. *We could order* pizza. (*simple sentences*)
           S.   V.   S.   V.

We could eat healthfully, *or* we could order pizza. (*compound sentence*)
    SIMPLE SENTENCE   CONJ.   SIMPLE SENTENCE

ACTIVITY 4 _____

Use *and, but,* or *or* to combine each pair of simple sentences into a compound sentence. Remember to use a comma before the conjunction.

Samples:

a. Miriam ran for class president. Gene ran for treasurer.

_____ Miriam ran for class president, and Gene ran for treasurer._____

b. I was saving for a watch. I spent the money on shoes.

_____ I was saving for a watch, but I spent the money on shoes._____

c. The bleachers should be repaired. They should be replaced.

_____ The bleachers should be repaired, or they should be replaced._____

1. You should shut the windows. The rain will get in.

   _____

2. The computer crashed. I lost my document.

   _____

3. In band, Edith plays trumpet. Horace plays drums.

   _____

4. Hilda suggested a movie. Brad wanted to play miniature golf.

   _____

5. This tire must be patched. It will go flat.

   _____

6. I read teen magazines. I don't believe everything they say.

   _____

7. The printer has a paper jam. Nobody can fix it.

   _____

8. Gloria wrote the song. Jessie performed it.

   _____

9. Send me an e-mail. Give me a call.

   _____

10. The sun is out. The temperature is still chilly.

   _____

 Writing Application Using Conjunctions

When is it okay to tell a secret that you agreed to keep, well, *secret*?

On a separate sheet of paper, write a paragraph of at least **five** sentences explaining your answer to this question. Use at least **three** conjunctions, and circle each one.

14 Interjections

Interjections help us interject, or add, sudden strong feelings to our sentences.

 An *interjection* is a word or short expression that shows sudden strong feeling.

The interjection is one of the eight parts of speech. However, the interjection is not part of the grammatical structure of the sentence. Its only job is to express strong feeling.

Ouch! That's hot.
INTERJ.

Hey! What are you doing?
INTERJ.

Wow! I am impressed!
INTERJ.

In the examples above, notice that each interjection is separated from the sentence by a mark of punctuation. Since an interjection expresses strong feeling, an exclamation point usually follows it, as in the examples above. If the interjection is more mild, a comma may follow it.

Oh, I don't know.

Well, that settles it.

Words commonly used as interjections include the following:

ah	oops	well
hey	ouch	whew
hooray	ugh	wow
oh	um	yikes
oh my		

Composition Hint

Even though some profane (so-called four-letter) words qualify as interjections, these words are not appropriate in your writing for school or business. Therefore, as you complete exercises in this book, use interjections that will not give offense.

ACTIVITY 1

What would you say in each of the following situations? Choose your answer from the suggested replies at the end of the exercise and write it on the line provided.

Sample:

You narrowly escape being tardy to class.

 Whew! That was close.

1. You win a contest.

   Hooray! I won!

2. You accidentally bang your knee on your desk.

   Ouch! That really hurt.

3. You reluctantly agree to lend your brother a shirt.

   Oh, I suppose you can borrow it.

4. You knock a porcelain figurine off a store shelf.

   Oops! Now I'll have to pay for that.

5. You step on slimy chewing gum with your bare foot.

   Ugh! That feels disgusting.

SUGGESTED REPLIES

Oops! Now I'll have to pay for that.
Oh, I suppose you can borrow it.
Ugh! That feels disgusting.

Hooray! I won!
Um, what did you say?
Ouch! That really hurt.

ACTIVITY 2

What would you say in each of the following situations? Use an interjection to write your own response. Choose your interjections from the list on page 122.

Sample:

You suddenly remember the name of a song that's been in your head all day.

Ah! Now I remember the name of that song.

1. You see a spider on your foot.

   Oh my! a spider on my foot

2. You accidentally bump into someone in the hallway.

3. You finish first in a race.

4. You see your friend across the street.

5. The teacher says, "Put down your pencils," *right* when you finish your test.

6. You reluctantly agree to pick up your little sister at her school.

_____

7. Your friend finds a twenty-dollar-bill on the sidewalk.

_____

8. Beads of sweat rolling down your forehead remind you how hot you are.

_____

9. You discover you grabbed your bother's lunch by mistake—a peanut butter-and-bologna sandwich.

_____

10. You accidentally walk into the wrong gender bathroom at school.

_____

ACTIVITY 3 _____

Young people often make up their own, unique interjections, such as _Awesome!_ and _Phat!_ In the space below, brainstorm unique interjections that you and your friends use. Then use five of these interjections to write sentences on the lines provided. One interjection and sentence are provided for you as samples.

```
                        Unique Interjections

        awesome



```

Sample:

_____ Awesome! Did you see that back flip? _____

1. _____

2. _____

3. _____

4. _____

5. _____

Review of Prepositions, Conjunctions, and Interjections

- **Prepositions** relate nouns or pronouns to some other part of the sentence.
- **Conjunctions** connect other words or word groups.
- **Interjections** show sudden strong feeling.

ACTIVITY 1

Read the passage (sentences have been numbered). Underline each *prepositional phrase*. Then, on the lines provided for each sentence, write the *preposition* and the *object of the preposition*. If a sentence does not have a prepositional phrase, write *none* on the line. Two items are completed as samples.

[1]If you were president, what changes would you make <u>in our nation</u>? [2]Perhaps you would sponsor campaigns in high schools to encourage voting among teenagers. [3]Would you lower the legal voting age to sixteen?

[4]Maybe your interests are more controversial. [5]What do you think about laws that control firearms? [6]Are they too strict, or not strict enough?

[7]Since teenagers often work for minimum wage, perhaps you would reform wage laws. [8]What do you think is a fair minimum wage? [9]What about classes that prepare young people for specific professions? [10]Should high schools teach mechanics, plumbing, cosmetology, professional cooking, etc.? [11]Or do you think these skills should be learned *after* high school graduation?

[12]In general, young people are interested in many of the same issues that interest older people. [13]Some of these issues are controversial, while others are more mundane. [14]No matter what the topic, teens have opinions about them. [15]Often, these opinions are surprisingly original.

	PREP.	OBJ. OF PREP.
1.	in	nation
2.		
3.		
4.	none	
5.		
6.		
7.		

8. _____   _____

9. _____   _____
   _____   _____

10. _____   _____

11. _____   _____

12. _____   _____
    _____   _____
    _____   _____

13. _____   _____

14. _____   _____

15. _____   _____

✏️ Writing
Application   Using Prepositional Phrases

If you were president, what is one change you would make in our nation? On a separate sheet of paper, write a paragraph of at least **five** sentences explaining why you would make this change. Use at least **three** prepositional phrases, and underline each one.

ACTIVITY 2

Follow the instructions below to write sentences using conjunctions.

Samples:

a. Use *or* to connect adverbs.

Did you clean your room quickly or slowly?

b. Use *and* to connect nouns and/or pronouns.

Elaine and I did homework together.

c. Use *but* to connect adjectives.

The officer was firm but polite.

1. Use *and* to connect adverbs.

_____

2. Use *or* to connect nouns and/or pronouns.

_____

3. Use *and* to connect verbs.

_____

4. Use *but* to connect adjectives.

_____

5. Use *or* to connect prepositional phrases.

_____

6. Use *and* to connect nouns and/or pronouns.

_____

7. Use *but* to connect adverbs.

_____

8. Use *and* to connect prepositional phrases.

_____

9. Use *or* to connect verbs.

_____

10. Use *or* to connect adjectives.

_____

ACTIVITY 3 _____

Use *and, but,* or *or* to combine each pair of simple sentences into one compound sentence.

> **Sample:**
>
> Hallie built a sandcastle. The tide washed it away.
>
> Hallie built a sandcastle, but the tide washed it away.

1. We could study math. We could play basketball.

_____

2. I aimed for the parking slot. I hit the fire hydrant.

_____

3. This is my outline. This is my essay.

_____

4. A spider waited. No insect flew into the web.

_____

5. Get a permission slip. You cannot go on the field trip.

_____

ACTIVITY 4 _____

Add an interjection to each of the following sentences, in keeping with the mood suggested in the parentheses following the sentence. Be sure to add an exclamation point or comma, as appropriate.

> **Sample:**
>
> _____ _Oh no!_ _____ I just dropped the pie. _(dismay)_

1. _____ I didn't expect to see you. _(surprise)_

2. _____ We nearly missed the bus. _(relief)_

3. _____ My boss gave me a raise. _(excitement)_

4. _____ Stop right there! _(urgency)_

5. _____ He ate the bread that fell on the floor. _(disgust)_

For Activity 5, read the following poems.

A Lament
Percy Bysshe Shelley

O world! O life! O time!

On whose last steps I climb,

    Trembling at that where I had stood before;

When will return the glory of your prime?

    No more—Oh, never more!

Out of the day and night

A joy has taken flight;

    Fresh spring, and summer, and winter hoar,[1]

Move my faint heart with grief, but with delight

    No more—Oh, never more!

[1]_hoar_: frost

from **The Eve of St. Agnes**
John Keats

> "Ah, Porphyro!" said she, "but even now
>
> Thy voice was at sweet tremble in mine ear,
>
> Made tuneable with every sweetest vow;
>
> And those sad eyes were spiritual and clear:
>
> How chang'd thou art! how pallid, chill, and drear!
>
> Give me that voice again, my Porphyro,
>
> Those looks immortal, those complainings dear!
>
> Oh leave me not in this eternal woe,
>
> For if thou diest, my love, I know not where to go."

ACTIVITY 5 _____

Refer to the poems to complete each task below.

1. What interjection does Shelley use in his poem? _____

2. How many times does Shelley use this interjection in the poem? _____

3. Why do you think Shelley uses the interjection numerous times?

   _____

   _____

   _____

4. What *two* interjections does Keats use in his poem? _____ and _____

5. What kind of emotion does Keats express with the first interjection you listed in item 4?

   _____

6. What kind of emotion does Keats express with the second interjection you listed in item 4?

   _____

7. Both poets use interjections to express emotion. Why do you think a poet would use a single word—an interjection—to express an emotion instead of describing that emotion with lots of words?

   _____

   _____

   _____

   _____

   _____

8. Shelley and Keats are among the Romantic poets—English poets who wrote during the Romantic peri-od of literature, from about 1785 to 1830. These writers valued *imagination, feelings,* and *personal expression,* among other things. Judging from the two poems above, how do you think the use of inter-jections helped Shelley and/or Keats demonstrate these Romantic values? Write your answer in com-plete sentences on the lines below.

_____

_____

_____

_____

_____

Review of the Eight Parts of Speech

Recall the eight parts of speech:
- noun
- pronoun
- verb
- adjective
- adverb
- preposition
- conjunction
- interjection

Read this excerpt from "Rappaccini's Daughter," a short story by Nathaniel Hawthorne. (The sentences have been numbered.) In the story, a young man named Giovanni observes Rappaccini's daughter, Beatrice, from a high window. After reading the passage, complete the activities that follow.

1 . . . the beautiful daughter of Rappaccini plucked one of the richest blossoms of the shrub, and was about to fasten it in her bosom. **2**But now . . . a singular incident occurred. **3**A small orange-colored reptile, of the lizard or chameleon species, chanced to be creeping along the path, just at the feet of Beatrice. **4**It appeared to Giovanni—but, at the distance from which he gazed, he could scarcely have seen anything so minute[1]—it appeared to him, however, that a drop or two of moisture from the broken stem of the flower descended upon the lizard's head. **5**For an instant the reptile contorted itself violently, and then lay motionless in the sunshine. **6**Beatrice observed this remarkable phenomenon . . . without surprise; nor did she therefore hesitate to arrange the fatal flower in her bosom.

[1]*minute:* tiny

ACTIVITY 1

Use the passage to do each task below.

1. On the lines below, list three *proper nouns* used in the passage.

    _____   _____   _____

2. On the lines below, list 15 *common nouns* used in the passage.

    _____   _____   _____

    _____   _____   _____

    _____   _____   _____

    _____   _____   _____

    _____   _____   _____

3. On the lines below, list five *pronouns* used in the passage.

    _____   _____   _____   _____   _____

Using Common and Proper Nouns

The great thing about nouns is that they're endlessly recyclable. Just mix them up and toss them into new sentences, and the same old nouns communicate new ideas, images, and information.

On a separate sheet of paper, use **ten** nouns from the passage to write **ten** original sentences of your own. Use at least one proper noun, and feel free to include additional nouns as well. Underline each common noun <u>once</u> and underline each proper noun <u>twice</u>.

Using Pronouns

What does Giovanni probably think of Beatrice after she shows no surprise at the lizard's death and wears the flower that killed the creature?

On a separate sheet of paper, write a paragraph of at least **five** sentences in response to this question. Underline each pronoun in your response.

ACTIVITY 2 _____

Use the passage to do each task below.

1. a. What is the verb in sentence 2? _____

   b. Is this verb an action verb or a linking verb? _____

   c. Explain how you know whether the verb is an action verb or a linking verb.

   _____

   _____

2. The verb *appeared* is used twice in sentence 4. On the lines below, use *appeared* in sentences of your own, first as an action verb and then as a linking verb.

   a. *action verb:* _____

   b. *linking verb:* _____

3. The word *surprise* is used as a noun in sentence 6. On the lines below, use *surprise* as a *verb* in a sentence of your own.

   _____

   _____

4. Finish writing each sentence below to complete the summary of the passage. Underline each verb in your sentences.

   a. First, Beatrice _____ .

   b. Next, the lizard _____ .

c. Then, moisture from the flower _____.

d. The lizard _____.

e. After that, Beatrice _____.

ACTIVITY 3 _____

Using the passage, write each adverb in the sentences listed below. (Sentences 4 and 5 each have two adverbs.) Then write the word or word group the adverb modifies, and the part of speech of that word/word group.

ADVERB
　　　　　　　　　　　　　　　　　　　　　WORD(S) MODIFIED AND PART OF SPEECH

1. Sentence 2: _____　　　　_____

2. Sentence 4: **a.** _____　　　　_____

　　　　　　　　b. _____　　　　_____

3. Sentence 5: **a.** _____　　　　_____

　　　　　　　　b. _____　　　　_____

ACTIVITY 4 _____

Using the passage, write each adjective in the sentences listed below. Then write the word the adjective modifies and the part of speech of that word.

ADJECTIVE
　　　　　　　　　　　　　　　　　　　　　WORD MODIFIED AND PART OF SPEECH

1. Sentence 1: **a.** _____　　　　_____

　　　　　　　　b. _____　　　　_____

2. Sentence 2: _____　　　　_____

3. Sentence 4: **a.** _____　　　　_____

　　　　　　　　b. _____　　　　_____

　　　　　　　　c. _____　　　　_____

✎ Writing
Application
　　　　　　　Using Adverbs and Adjectives

How would you react if you plucked a beautiful flower and then suddenly realized it was deadly? On a separate sheet of paper, write at least **three** sentences telling how you would react. Use at least **two adverbs** and **two adjectives.** Underline each adverb <u>once</u> and draw an arrow from it to the word or word group it modifies. Underline each adjective <u>twice</u> and draw an arrow from it to the word it modifies.

Underline each prepositional phrase in the passage. (There are 20.)

ACTIVITY 6 _____

Use the passage to do each task below.

1. In the final sentence in the passage, Hawthorne uses the conjunction *nor.* (*Nor* is not commonly in our everyday speech; like *or,* it is used to join options or alternatives.) In the passage, circle *nor* and the four other conjunctions, for a total of five conjunctions.

2. Write five original sentences using conjunctions, as directed below.

   a. Use *and* to connect adjectives.

   _____

   b. Use *but* to connect adverbs.

   _____

   c. Use *or* to connect nouns and/or pronouns.

   _____

   d. Use *and* to connect prepositional phrases.

   _____

   e. Use *or* to connect verbs.

   _____

 Writing
Application

Using Prepositional Phrases
and Interjections

In the excerpt above, Giovanni does not speak to Beatrice. If he did speak, what do you think he would say?

On a separate sheet of paper, write **three** or more sentences you imagine Giovanni might say to either Beatrice or himself. Use at least **three prepositional phrases** and **one interjection**. Underline the prepositional phrases and circle the interjection(s).

Parts of Speech

It's time to take a break from traditional grammar exercises. The following activities ask you to explore how people use the eight parts of speech in the real world, outside your classroom walls. Which activity sparks your interest? Choose an activity to complete; then, with your teacher's approval, share the results with your classmates. Have a good time!

Engine Fuel

An Internet search engine scours the World Wide Web for specific words that a user types in. If you think of these words as fuel for the engine, what part of speech fuels search engines best? Conduct at least ten different searches on the Internet, trying out different parts of speech in the search field and evaluating the results. In addition, poll friends and family members for recently used search terms. Write up a list of all these search terms and their parts of speech. Then answer these questions: In search engines, do people tend to use one part of speech more than any other? Why?

I'm Stuck on You

Has anyone ever been *stuck on you*? What does that mean, anyway? This phrase is an *idiom*—an expression whose meaning is not based on the combined meanings of its words. English speakers learn to use idioms simply by hearing them used. Like the phrase above, many idioms rely on prepositions to express an idea. How many idioms using prepositions can you collect? Here are a couple more to get you started: *It's water under the bridge. I'll go out with a bang.*

Cover Story

Imagine that you are launching a new magazine aimed at young adult readers. Pick a theme (sports, fashion, entertainment, etc.) and design a cover for the first issue. Use all eight parts of speech in cover text to attract readers. Make a mock-up of your magazine cover (clip graphics from old magazines or create your own). Mount the cover on poster board. Then, on the poster around the cover's edges, label the parts of speech used in each headline.

¿Habla Español?

Do you speak a language besides English? Compare how English and another language use the parts of speech. For example, in English, an adjective almost always come before the word it modifies. But in Spanish, an adjective may follow the word it modifies. Compare the two languages' uses of some or all of the eight parts of speech. Provide examples in both languages to illustrate the comparisons.

May I Take Your Order?

Choose a trade or profession that interests you. Which part or parts of speech are especially important in this line of work? For example, cooks rely on verbs: *measure* the flour; *bake* the fish. Advertisers rely on adjectives: *effective* cleanser; *smooth, quiet* ride. A preschool teacher may use lots of interjections: *Wow!* What a great job! Explain how one or two parts of speech are especially important to a particular line of work and give examples to illustrate your point.

Gone but Not Forgotten

Many historical and literary figures are memorable not just as a single individual but as half of a notable pair—two names joined by the conjunction *and.* Think of Romeo and Juliet, Antony and Cleopatra, and the Greeks and Trojans. Make a list of as many notable pairs as you can think of—including modern pairs, such as Batman and Robin. Make a time line showing each pair's place in history, whether real or fictional.

Adverb Seeks Adjective

If you were a part of speech, which would you be? Are you active like a verb? Impulsive like an interjection? Do you like things neatly categorized, like a noun? Write short descriptions of each part of speech as though it were a person. Then identify the part you most identify with and explain the traits you have that inspired you to choose that part of speech.

Ripped from the Headlines

Have you ever noticed that newspaper headlines are rarely complete sentences? Which parts of speech do headlines use most? Which parts are used least often? Make a poster showing different kinds of headlines (short, long, front-page, back-page, business, lifestyle, etc.) that you've clipped from newspapers. Label the parts of speech in each headline. Then write an explanation of why, in your opinion, a headline is rarely an entire sentence.

Parts of Speech

PART 1

Directions: Look at the item with the same number as the underlined part. Circle the letter of the best replacement for the underlined part. If the current part is best, circle *A* or *F* for *NO CHANGE*.

Catherine and Antwon took <u>his</u> world cultures tests late.
1

<u>C</u> **1. A.** NO CHANGE
    B. her
    C. their
    D. there

I asked <u>specific</u> for a diet soda.
2

<u>G</u> **2. F.** NO CHANGE
    G. specifically
    H. specificity
    J. in a specific manner

The expensive hotel used <u>Italian</u> marble for the countertops.
3

_____ **3. A.** NO CHANGE
    B. italian
    C. italy
    D. Italy

That old boat motor sounds <u>really loudly</u>.
4

_____ **4. F.** NO CHANGE
    G. real loud
    H. real loudly
    J. really loud

Grizzly bears may look cuddly, <u>and</u> they are dangerous.
5

_____ **5. A.** NO CHANGE
    B. or
    C. for
    D. but

<u>Phew what</u> stinks in here?
6

_____ **6. F.** NO CHANGE
    G. Phew What
    H. Phew! What
    J. Phew. What

The message Blair wrote in my yearbook was <u>thoughtful sweet</u>.
7

_____ **7. A.** NO CHANGE
    B. thoughtful and sweet
    C. thoughtful but sweet
    D. thoughtful or sweet

The <u>state of Arizona</u> may get its name from the Pima

8
Indian word *Arizuma*.

8. **F.** NO CHANGE
   G. State of Arizona
   H. state of arizona
   J. state

I went to <u>you're</u> house, but you weren't there.

9

9. **A.** NO CHANGE
   B. youre
   C. your
   D. your'

The bouquet of roses was <u>surprised</u>.

10

10. **F.** NO CHANGE
    G. a surprise
    H. surprisingly
    J. in a surprising way

Lately, Amanda <u>been calling</u> me every day.

11

11. **A.** NO CHANGE
    B. be calling
    C. calling
    D. has been calling

Together, the sisters <u>selected and purchased</u> a CD by
their favorite band.

12

12. **F.** NO CHANGE
    G. selected, purchased
    H. selected or purchased
    J. selected but purchased

<u>What did you pack our lunches in?</u>

13

13. **A.** NO CHANGE
    B. What did you pack our lunches
    C. In what did you pack our lunches
    D. What did you pack in our lunches

You should give a tip <u>the delivery person</u>.

14

14. **F.** NO CHANGE
    G. for the delivery person
    H. to the delivery person
    J. from the delivery person

When I asked for volunteers, Garth raised his hand
<u>in a quick manner</u>.

15

15. **A.** NO CHANGE
    B. quick
    C. quickely
    D. quickly

Directions: In each item, certain parts are underlined and labeled. Circle the letter of the underlined part that contains an error. If the item has no error, circle *E* for *No error.*

_____ 16. <u>Honoré de Balzac</u> was a <u>French</u> novelist who wrote more than 90 novels <u>and</u>
     A   **B**   **C**

   short stories <u>during</u> the nineteenth century. <u>No error</u>
         D   **E**

_____ 17. The <u>bobcat</u>, which is a <u>vicious</u> wild animal, <u>have</u> a short tail, reddish-brown hair,
      A   **B**   **C**

   <u>and</u> black spots. <u>No error</u>
   D   **E**

_____ 18. The <u>talent show</u>, which <u>had scheduled</u> for mid-October, <u>has now been postponed</u>
      A   **B**   **C**

   until <u>January</u>. <u>No error</u>
      D   **E**

_____ 19. <u>Its</u> humiliating when <u>I</u> am <u>in front of</u> the class but <u>can't</u> work the algebra problem
   A   **B** **C**   **D**

   on the chalkboard. <u>No error</u>
          E

_____ 20. Huey is the new student in homeroom, <u>but</u> I <u>don't know</u> where <u>he</u> transferred <u>from</u>.
               A   **B**   **C**   **D**

   <u>No error</u>
   E

_____ 21. Give <u>Wendy</u> the directions, <u>but</u> she <u>can</u> drive us <u>there</u>. <u>No error</u>
     A   **B**   **C**   **D** **E**

_____ 22. <u>Isnt</u> Ellis Bell the pen name <u>of Emily Brontë</u>, the <u>English</u> author who <u>wrote</u>
   A   **B**   **C**   **D**

   Wuthering Heights? <u>No error</u>
          E

_____ 23. <u>Unfortunate</u>, Gregor <u>sneaked</u> into the maintenance room, and <u>he</u> set off the
   A   **B**   **C**

   sprinklers on the football field <u>during</u> the middle of the game. <u>No error</u>
               D   **E**

_____ 24. <u>You'll</u> need to walk really <u>careful</u> over the rope bridge because <u>it</u> is old <u>and</u> weak.
   A   **B**   **C**   **D**

   <u>No error</u>
   E

_____ 25. <u>Ouch!</u> I <u>glanced</u> away for a moment and <u>shut</u> my thumb in my locker door by
   A **B**   **C**

   <u>accidentally</u>. <u>No error</u>
   D   **E**

2 Punctuation

You learned about the parts of speech and grammar in Part One. Now we come to Part Two, which focuses on punctuation. Like the eight parts of speech, the marks of punctuation help us express our exact thoughts, feelings, and ideas in writing.

In standard written English, rules govern the use of punctuation. In the following lessons, you will review these rules, particularly as they pertain to

the **period** [**.**]

the **question mark** [**?**]

the **exclamation point** [**!**]

the **comma** [**,**]

the **semicolon** [**;**]

the **colon** [**:**]

the **apostrophe** [**'**]

quotation marks [**"..."**]

the **punctuation of titles**

17 End Punctuation

A complete sentence ends in one of three punctuation marks: **period, question mark,** or **exclamation point.** Depending on the end mark used, a sentence carries a particular tone and meaning. Consider the different effects created in the sentence below, just by changing the end mark.

You cut your hair**.**

You cut your hair**?**

You cut your hair**!**

Each end mark has one or more main uses.

END MARK	USED WITH	EXAMPLE
. (period)	statements	*I want to go to the mall.*
	polite requests	*Please drive me to the mall.*
	commands	*Drop me off at the main entrance.*
? (question mark)	inquiries	*May I borrow twenty dollars?*
! (exclamation point)	strong feeling	*Oh! I lost my wallet!*
	urgent commands	*Stop that thief!*

ACTIVITY 1

Add an end mark to each sentence to best express its meaning and tone.

Samples:

a. Which one of these is the salad fork ___?___

b. What an amazing time we had at the lake ___!___

1. Mary Cassatt, an American artist, painted scenes of domestic life _____

2. Please fix me a cup of hot cocoa with marshmallows in it _____

3. What are your plans for spring break this year _____

4. Our team just won the championship _____

5. Mom, may a couple of my friends sleep over on Friday night _____

6. Place your book reports in the basket on my desk _____

7. In 1872, Susan B. Anthony was arrested simply for voting _____

8. Something is on fire in the kitchen _____

9. I plan to become a professional race-car driver someday _____

10. Don't you dare say another word _____

18 The Comma

The comma can serve a variety of purposes within a sentence. Study the rules below to learn the main uses of commas.

 1. Use a comma before a coordinating conjunction that joins sentences.

Coordinating conjunctions include *and, but, or, nor, for,* and *yet*.

Rudy signed up for shop class, *but* I chose computer programming.

 2. Use a comma to separate items in a series.

The terrarium includes *rocks, a water dish, a heat lamp, and a turtle*. (a series of nouns)

Raul *can sing, dance, and act* with impressive skill. (a series of verbs)

Niccolo's latest painting is *large, colorful, and unique*. (a series of adjectives)

Paint splattered *on my shirt, on the counter, and on Mrs. Jerrod*. (a series of prepositional phrases)

When you include only two items in a row (two nouns, two verbs, etc.), you should not use a comma between them. Simply use a conjunction such as *and, but,* or *or*.

Niccolo's latest painting is *large and colorful*. (NOT *large, and colorful*)

Paint splattered *on my shirt and on the counter*. (NOT *on my shirt, and on the counter*)

 3. Use a comma after certain introductory words and word groups.

Yes, Annie will babysit Lindsay tomorrow.

Because of heavy rain, the game was postponed.

 4. Use commas to set off most interrupting words and expressions.

Audrey, welcome to our home. (noun of direct address)

Welcome, *Audrey*, to our home. (noun of direct address)

Mercury, *the planet nearest the sun*, rotates very slowly. (appositive)

(An appositive follows a noun or pronoun and renames or explains it.)

Venus, *however*, is nearest Earth. (interrupting word)

Your secret admirer is Benson, *not Denny*. (interrupting expression)

Note: To learn how to use commas with direct quotations, look on page 156 in Lesson 21.

Insert commas, as appropriate, in each of the following sentences.

> **Samples:**
>
> **a.** Good sources of carbohydrates are wheat bread, pasta, and oatmeal.
>
> **b.** To her surprise, she won the costume contest.
>
> **c.** The numbat, a type of anteater, is an endangered species.

1. The toad an amphibian is usually covered in warts.

2. We'll need rice broccoli cheese and mushrooms for the casserole.

3. After three hours in front of the computer my eyes ached.

4. A long dark tunnel led into the cool cave.

5. Calcium builds your teeth and bones and iron builds rich blood.

6. The treasure hunt led us over the hill beneath an oak tree and next to a boulder.

7. I am happy to meet you Mr. Aimes.

8. The cerebrum not the cerebellum is the largest part of the brain.

9. Press the button or the elevator will never come.

10. No my cell phone did not ring during the biology midterm.

Composition Hint

When two or more adjectives precede a noun or pronoun, a comma is often—but not always—necessary. If you can switch the order of the adjectives, or you can replace each comma with *and*, then the commas are necessary.

> It was a *joyous*, *tearful* reunion. (necessary comma)
>
> I'll wear the *old red* shirt. (no comma necessary)

Using commas as needed, write sentences that use two or more adjectives to modify any five of the following nouns.

holiday	actor	lipstick	boots	idea
stereo	spy	jacket	song	athlete

1. _____

2. _____

3. _____

4. _____

5. _____

Another Composition Hint

Speech patterns do not always reflect the rules of comma usage. For this reason, don't add a comma to a sentence just because you would pause there when speaking. Instead, rely on the rules for comma usage.

INSTEAD OF: Douglas Adams wrote *The Long Dark Tea-Time of the Soul*, and *The Hitchhiker's Guide to the Galaxy*.

WRITE: Douglas Adams wrote *The Long Dark Tea-Time of the Soul* and *The Hitchhiker's Guide to the Galaxy*. (no comma between the two direct objects)

ACTIVITY 3

Insert commas, as appropriate, in each of the following sentences. Some sentences do not need commas.

1. I went bike riding with Kerry my new best friend on Saturday afternoon.

2. Ollie's jokes were not very funny yet everyone laughed.

3. The soothing classical music put me to sleep.

4. The academic program not the sports program attracted me to the state university.

5. Hailey wrote her entire history term paper on Friday night and spent the rest of the weekend with her friends.

6. After an hour of band practice everyone was ready for a break.

7. A tackle box fishing rods and a can of worms rattled around in the back of the pickup.

8. The strange honking sound unfortunately for me was my own snoring.

9. Gerry sent her class photo to all of her relatives and to everyone she had met at camp.

10. His exotic sultry accent captivated me immediately.

11. As I was telling you Camille Africa is a continent not a country.

12. My sister plans to become a marine scientist a chemist or a biologist.

13. Alexander read *Dr. Wildlife: The Crusade of a Northwoods Veterinarian* and *A Midsummer Night's Dream*.

14. The hero in the story could leap tall buildings in a single bound and fly through the air like a supersonic jet.

15. Yes I am interested in the volunteer program but I have not signed up for it yet.

19 The Semicolon and the Colon

We use the **semicolon** to signal a brief pause that is longer than a pause for a comma but not as long as that for a period. We use the **colon** to point the reader's attention ahead to a list or some other "announced" word or word group.

The Semicolon (;)

 1. Use a semicolon to join sentences that are not connected by a coordinating conjunction.

A semicolon joins the following sentences, not a conjunction such as *and* or *but*.

Hot-air balloons filled the sky; it was the annual Balloon Fest.

This story is about a teenage girl; she enters a sled-dog race.

Toby had never tasted a kumquat; he didn't even know what it was.

Do not use a semicolon to join clauses that are not closely related in meaning.

Hot-air balloons filled the sky. We searched for a parking spot near the festival.

This story is about a teenage girl. Actually, I would rather read about sports.

Toby had never tasted a kumquat. His mom bought a bag of these citrus fruits to make jam.

ACTIVITY 1

Decide whether a semicolon belongs in each sentence. On the line provided, write *no* if no semicolon is needed. If a semicolon is needed, write *yes* on the line and insert a semicolon where it belongs in the sentence.

Samples:

___yes___ **a.** Malaria is caused by blood parasites; mosquitoes transmit them.

___no___ **b.** Meredith brought a picnic lunch, and Lee brought a beach ball.

_____ **1.** Napoléon Bonaparte was nicknamed The Little Corporal he was about five and a half feet tall.

_____ **2.** The written text was helpful, but the maps were more helpful.

_____ **3.** You mark the pumpkin I'll carve the face.

_____ **4.** Pulp fiction is slang for "popular literature" the category includes spy thrillers, mysteries, science fiction, and more.

_____ **5.** The book was about dinosaurs I've always been interested in the prehistoric period.

2. Use a semicolon to join sentences connected by a conjunctive adverb or transitional phrase.

I dislike fried eggs; *nevertheless*, I ate them to please Grandma.

Hot-air balloons filled the sky; *however*, Tad's balloon was not among them.

Tad arrived late; *as a result*, his balloon was last to launch.

Toby had never tasted a kumquat; *in fact*, he didn't even know what it was.

In the examples above, notice that the semicolon comes *before* the conjunctive adverb or transitional phrase, and a comma comes after the connector.

CONJUNCTIVE ADVERBS consequently, furthermore, however, instead, moreover, nevertheless, otherwise, therefore, thus

TRANSITIONAL PHRASES as a result, for instance, in fact, on the other hand, that is

ACTIVITY 2 _____

Join each pair of sentences with the connector in parentheses and the appropriate punctuation. Write your sentences on the lines provided.

> **Sample:**
>
> Lance is an affectionate brother. He is a loyal friend. *(moreover)*
>
> Lance is an affectionate brother; moreover, he is a loyal friend.

1. I got a job. I could afford the prom dress. *(as a result)*

_____

2. Pick up some milk. We can't eat cereal tomorrow. *(otherwise)*

_____

3. Liz's idea is great. Fred's is more realistic. *(however)*

_____

4. I passed the exam. I got a B+. *(in fact)*

_____

5. Don't cook. We'll go out. *(instead)*

_____

 3. Use a semicolon to join items in a series when one or more items have a comma.

We traveled to Phoenix, Arizona; Santa Fe, New Mexico; and Abilene, Texas.

On the stage stood Petra, the first-place winner; Kenton, the second-place winner; Mr. Cortes, the math teacher; and Ms. Nguyen, the principal.

Please bring the blue sweater, which is mine; the white sweater, which is Lara's; and the raincoat, which is Akeno's.

In each sentence, add one or more semicolons as necessary.

> **Sample:**
>
> Lucy sent graduation announcements to Ms. Percy, her favorite teacher; her grandparents; and her cousins.

1. My passions include Tae Kwon Do, a martial arts form swimming and singing.

2. Add the eggs the sugar, mixed with the baking soda and the vanilla.

3. The tour has stops in Johnstown, Colorado Toledo, Ohio and Manorville, New York.

4. Marian Evans, whose pen name was George Eliot Matthew Arnold and Christina Rossetti are on the syllabus.

5. We studied ladybugs, which are beetles, actually butterflies and dragonflies.

ACTIVITY 4

Use semicolons in your own sentences, written on a separate sheet of paper. Follow the instructions below to write each sentence. You may want to look at the sentences in Activities 1–3 for ideas and examples.

1. Use a semicolon to join two closely related sentences.

2. Use a semicolon and the conjunctive adverb *however* to join two sentences.

3. Use a semicolon and any conjunctive adverb except *however* to join two sentences.

4. Use a semicolon and a transitional phrase to join two sentences.

5. Use semicolons to separate items in a series, making sure that at least one item in the series contains a comma.

The Colon (:)

 1. Use a colon to call attention to what follows.

My conclusion is this: rats understand English.

He had one endearing quality: a tendency to blush easily.

For the project you will need the following: litmus paper, a lemon, and milk.

Notice that a word such as *this* or an expression such as *the following* often precedes a colon. If these signal words are not present, the sentence may not need a colon, as in the following examples.

My conclusion is that rats understand English. (no colon)

For the project you will need litmus paper, a lemon, and milk. (no colon)

Similarly, a colon is not used when a series is introduced with "for example" or "namely."

For the project you will need a few everyday items, *for example,* a lemon and milk. (no colon)

2. Use a colon after the salutation in a formal or business letter.

Dear Dr. Thompson**:**

Dear Mrs. Vargas**:**

Dear Principal LeBeaux**:**

(*Note:* In an informal or friendly letter, a comma follows the salutation.)

ACTIVITY 5

In each sentence, insert a colon if it is needed. Some sentences do not need a colon.

> **Samples:**
>
> **a.** My opinion was blunt: "It's awful!"
>
> **b.** Leona does crafts such as beadwork, leatherworking, and woodworking. *(no colon)*

1. Campers should pack the following sleeping bag, change of clothing, and food.

2. She devised a creative solution patching the hole with chewing gum.

3. My answer is this maybe.

4. Our understanding was that the test had been rescheduled.

5. The instructions are as follows write your evaluation and seal it in an envelope.

6. The main ingredients are these pecans, eggs, syrup, and sugar.

7. For the class party you should bring one snack and one beverage.

8. At my birthday party I received a CD, a Yankees cap, and new shoes.

9. Party favors can be items such as these stickers, jelly beans, and party hats.

10. At the bake sale we sold many goodies, for example, muffins, granola bars, and cookies.

ACTIVITY 6

Write a colon or a comma after each salutation, as needed.

> **Samples:**
>
> **a.** Dear Mr. Wheatland:
>
> **b.** Dear Sammie:

1. Dear Professor Collins

2. Dear Grandma

3. Dear Sarah Beth

4. Dear Ms. Ingalls

5. Dear Chairman Keller

6. Dear Mom and Dad

7. Dear Sir or Madam

8. Dear Vice Principal Holt

9. Dear Mr. and Mrs. Velmont

10. Dear Uncle Adam

20 The Apostrophe

We use the apostrophe to make the possessive forms of words and to form contractions.

 1. Add an apostrophe and *s* to form the possessive of singular words and plurals that do not end in *s*.

SINGULAR WORDS: *man's* mustache, *book's* cover, *Charles's* house, *Ms. Jones's* car

PLURALS NOT ENDING IN *s*:   *men's* suits, *geese's* feathers, *feet's* odor, *mice's* nest

In the examples above, note that *Charles* and *Ms. Jones* are singular words, even though they end in an *s*. Since they are singular, they take an apostrophe and *s* to form the possessive.

 2. To form the possessive of plural words ending in *s,* add an apostrophe.

PLURAL WORDS: *teachers'* lounge, *students'* lockers, *books'* covers, the *Joneses'* car

 3. Use an apostrophe to form the possessive of indefinite pronouns but *not* personal pronouns.

INDEFINITE PRONOUNS: *someone's* hat, *nobody's* fault, *everyone's* friend

(NOT *her's* or *their's* or *it's*)

 4. Use an apostrophe in a contraction in place of the missing letter or letters.

CONTRACTIONS: shouldn't   they've   let's   hasn't   it's

ACTIVITY 1

On the line provided, write the possessive form of each word in parentheses.

Samples:

a. ____magazine's____ cover story (*magazine*)

b. ____ducks'____ offspring (*ducks*)

1. _____ bicycle (*somebody*)

2. _____ pyramids (*Egypt*)

3. _____ cost (*tires*)

4. _____ nest (*mice*)

5. _____ pronunciation (*word*)

6. _____ favorite *(no one)*

7. _____ maps *(atlas)*

8. _____ howl *(wolf)*

9. _____ traits *(mammals)*

10. _____ house *(Amy Martinez)*

11. _____ laces *(shoe)*

12. _____ price tag *(shoes)*

13. _____ lunches *(everybody)*

14. _____ toys *(children)*

15. _____ exhibits *(museum)*

Writing Application

Using the Possessive Forms of Nouns and Pronouns

Think about your group of friends. What stands out about each of these people? Maybe it is a personality trait, a talent, a possession, or an aspect of physical appearance.

Write **five** sentences identifying specific aspects of **five** friends. Use a possessive noun or pronoun in each sentence and underline it.

ACTIVITY 2

On the line provided, write the contraction of each pair of words.

Samples:

a. we have _____ *we've* _____

b. did not _____ *didn't* _____

1. she will _____

2. would not _____

3. you are _____

4. it is _____

5. are not _____

6. they are _____

7. is not _____

8. will not _____

9. let us _____

10. can not _____

Read the following stanza from "Home," a poem by Edgar A. Guest. Then do each task that follows, writing your responses on a separate sheet of paper. Except for item 3, write your answers in complete sentences.

It takes a heap o' livin' in a house t' make it home,

A heap o' sun an' shadder,[1] an' ye sometimes have t' roam

Afore ye really 'preciate the things ye lef' behind,

An' hunger fer 'em somehow, with 'em allus[2] on yer mind.

It don't make any differunce[3] how rich ye get t' be,

How much yer chairs an' tables cost, how great yer luxury;

It ain't home t' ye, though it be the palace of a king,

Until somehow yer soul is sort o' wrapped 'round everything.

[1]*shadder*: shadow

[2]*allus*: always

[3]*differunce*: difference

1. Guest uses apostrophes to form unusual contractions in "Home." After reading this stanza, why do you think he uses these contractions in the poem?

2. In line 7, Guest uses the slang contraction *ain't*. Why do you think he used this grammatically incorrect contraction, which educated writers pride themselves on *not* using?

3. Rewrite the poem using complete words instead of contractions. Underline each word or word pair in your version that was a contraction in Guest's poem.

4. Read the new version of "Home" you created in item 3, above. How is the mood of your version different from Guest's version? Use examples from the two poems to explain your answer.

5. Do you think readers would respond differently to your version of "Home" than to Guest's version? Use examples from the two versions to explain your answer.

21 Quotation Marks

We use quotation marks to enclose a speaker's exact words and to enclose certain titles. This lesson tells you how to use quotation marks with direct quotations, and Lesson 22 tells you how to use quotation marks with titles.

 Use quotation marks to enclose a speaker's exact words.

Quotation marks always come in pairs. If you have an opening quotation mark, you must have a closing quotation mark.

"Let's go to the lake this weekend," said Lamont.

Ms. Liu asked, "How many of you have read *Uncle Tom's Cabin?*"

"Hi," said Vasily.

Mary Wollstonecraft wrote, "The mind will ever be unstable that has only prejudices to rest on."

(a) A *direct quotation* shows the speaker's exact words. An *indirect quotation* does not. Therefore, use quotation marks only with *direct* quotations.

DIRECT QUOTE:	Dad said, "You are grounded for a week."
INDIRECT QUOTE:	Dad told me that I'm grounded for an entire week.
DIRECT QUOTE:	"Are you going to Leroy's party?" said Lizzie.
INDIRECT QUOTE:	Lizzie asked if you're going to Leroy's party.
DIRECT QUOTE:	Wollstonecraft wrote, "Strengthen the female mind by enlarging it."
INDIRECT QUOTE:	Wollstonecraft wrote that women should get an education.

(b) Quotation marks enclose only the person's exact words, not expressions like *he said*.

"Let's go to the lake this weekend," said Lamont, "and catch some fish."

"When you finish your test," announced Mr. Polaski, "turn it facedown on your desk."

"Hey, Troy!" shouted Joaquin. "Want to play basketball?"

(c) Place a comma after expressions like *he said* when they introduce a quotation.

Lamont said, "Let's go to the lake this weekend."

Mr. Polaski announced, "When you finish your test, turn it facedown on your desk."

Joaquin shouted, "Hey, Troy! Want to play basketball?"

ACTIVITY 1

Insert quotation marks in each sentence as needed. One sentence does not need quotation marks.

Samples:

a. "Ray Bradbury is my favorite writer," said André.

b. "When I blow the whistle," said Coach Anna, "begin your laps."

1. Kate said, We have to dissect frogs in biology class.

2. Matthew Arnold wrote, Journalism is literature in a hurry.

3. I'll see you at the dance, said John to Cassidy.

4. Ellen said that I can borrow her raincoat.

5. Oh, great, I said. This calculator needs batteries.

ACTIVITY 2

Rewrite each sentence, adding a comma and quotation marks where they are needed.

Sample:

Margo said Thank you, Brad.

_____Margo said, "Thank you, Brad."_____

1. Jane shouted Watch out for that tree!

_____

2. Someone muttered That's ridiculous.

_____

3. The newscaster said Stay tuned.

_____

4. He whispered Are you awake?

_____

5. I said I disagree with you.

_____

(d) Place a period or comma following a quotation *inside* the quotation marks.

"Let's go to the lake this weekend," said Lamont. "We'll catch some fish."

(e) Place a semicolon or colon *outside* quotation marks.

Wollstonecraft said writers like Rousseau "degrade one half of the human species"; she was referring to women.

She described "the most perfect education": one that teaches independence.

ACTIVITY 3

On the lines provided, rewrite each sentence. Add quotation marks exactly where they are needed.

> **Samples:**
>
> **a.** Heather said, I love this song.
>
> Heather said, "I love this song."
>
> **b.** Mom said, Someone help with the dishes; no one was listening.
>
> Mom said, "Someone help with the dishes"; no one was listening.

1. I have arrived, said Morton.

_____

2. The magician said, Watch this; we watched.

_____

3. Dad said, The school bus is here.

_____

4. Here's your notebook, said Petra.

_____

5. I was hoping, said Phil, that the rumor was true.

_____

ACTIVITY 4

Can you unscramble this quotation? With your teacher's approval, you may choose to work with a classmate to complete this activity.

Directions: Drop the letters from each vertical column—not necessarily in the order in which they appear—into the empty boxes below them to spell words. Use each letter only once. The quotation reads from left to right, line by line. Black squares indicate ends of words. Once you unscramble the quotation, write it on the lines provided, using quotation marks and a period.

B	M	O	N	M	T	O	G	W	R	W	T	E	T	E	V	E	R	Y
D	E	C	O	N	E	B	Y	A	T	H	R	T	I	E	R	E		
I	O	W	I	S	I	N		S		I	A	T		O	N			
														N	G			

	T									T							
									I								
		R															
				S					I								

Gerald Brenan wrote,

_____

_____

(f) Place a question mark or exclamation point *inside* the quotation mark if it is part of the quote. Place it *outside* if it is *not* part of the quotation.

I asked Lamont, "Why are you shouting?"

He said, "I caught a fish!"

Does Wollstonecraft call some adults "overgrown children"?

(The question mark is not part of the quotation.)

I laughed when I read about "overgrown children"!

(The entire sentence, not the quoted words, is an exclamation.)

ACTIVITY 5

Decide whether the quotation marks in each sentence are placed correctly. On the line provided, write *C* for *correct* or *I* for *incorrect*.

Samples:

_C_ **a.** Have you heard that pork is "the other white meat"?

_I_ **b.** The fans shouted, "Go, Cubs"!

_____ **1.** "I won!" said Deena.

_____ **2.** Anthony said, "Who invited you"?

_____ **3.** Class photos will be taken tomorrow", Ms. Vickers said.

_____ **4.** What did he mean when he said "once in a blue moon"?

_____ 5. "Over here"! shouted Jessica, waving at me.

_____ 6. Ernesto said, "This biography of John Muir is interesting".

_____ 7. "Can we get a puppy?" I asked Mom.

_____ 8. "When you take out the trash," said Dad, "close the lid securely."

_____ 9. "After my winning basket", said Phina, "everyone applauded!"

_____ 10. "Your English essays are due by Friday", said Mr. Carson.

ACTIVITY 6 _____

On a separate sheet of paper, rewrite each sentence marked *incorrect* in Activity 4. Place quotation marks correctly.

 Writing Application

Using Quotation Marks

When was the last time you had a disagreement with a friend, teacher, or family member? What did you and the other person say to each other?

On a separate sheet of paper, write a short dialogue (ten sentences or so) between two people who are disagreeing about something. Use quotation marks to enclose the words of each speaker. Place marks of punctuation inside or outside the quotation marks, as appropriate.

22 Punctuating Titles

We use quotation marks and italics to punctuate titles. When you write by hand, use underlining instead of *italics*.

 1. Use quotation marks to enclose the titles of short works.

SHORT STORIES:	"A White Heron"	"The Far and the Near"
POEMS:	"The Road Not Taken"	"The Streets of Laredo"
SONGS:	"What a Wonderful World"	"Hammer and a Nail"
ARTICLES:	"A New Mission to Mars"	"How to Pan for Gold"
CHAPTERS:	"The Structure of Cells"	"How to Punctuate Titles"

 2. Use italics with the titles of longer works.

When you write by hand, use underlining instead of italics.

BOOKS	*Crispin: The Cross of Lead*	Literature in Colonial America
PLAYS	*Our Town*	The Crucible
FILMS	*The Terminator*	How to Lose a Guy in Ten Days
MAGAZINES	*Teen People*	Baseball Digest
NEWSPAPERS	*The New York Times*	The Dallas Morning News
MUSIC CDS	*Come Away with Me*	America Town

Note: To learn how to capitalize titles, turn to page 176 in Lesson 24.

ACTIVITY 1

Use quotation marks or underlining to punctuate each title, as appropriate.

> **Samples:**
>
> **a.** Ms. Tartuff read from an article called "Shakespeare's Ghost Writers."
>
> **b.** Jacob Have I Loved is a novel about sibling rivalry.

1. My older sister is trying out for a part in Bye Bye Birdie.

2. Keiko enjoys listening to Stevie Ray Vaughan's album Live at Carnegie Hall.

3. Of all the stories Edgar Allan Poe wrote, I like The Fall of the House of Usher best.

4. Josh Groban sings a beautiful song called You're Still You.

5. Please turn to Chapter Six, Foundations of American Government.

6. Do you subscribe to Seventeen or Sports Illustrated?

7. The Blind Men and the Elephant is a humorous poem by John Godfrey Saxe.

8. Each weekend, Mom reads USA Today, slowly paging through each of the newspaper's sections.

9. I love Robert Cormier's books, such as The Chocolate War.

10. My friends and I watched The Wizard of Oz on DVD.

 Writing Application

Punctuating Titles

Top ten lists are always popular: the top ten teen films of all time, the top ten love songs of the year, the top ten books everyone should read—you get the idea.

Make your own top ten list called The Top Ten Books, Stories, and Music for Young People. Include titles from at least **seven** of these categories:

short story	poem	song	article	chapter	music CD
book	play	film	magazine	newspaper	

Write a sentence explaining why each item belongs in your top ten and punctuate the titles and sentences correctly.

23 Review of Punctuation

This review covers the following marks of punctuation:

the **period** [.]   the **comma** [,]   the **apostrophe** [']

the **question mark** [?]   the **semicolon** [;]   quotation **marks** ["..."]

the **exclamation point** [!]   the **colon** [:]   the **punctuation of titles**

ACTIVITY 1 _____

Carefully read the following passage, noticing which marks of punctuation are needed. Add end punctuation, commas, apostrophes, quotation marks, and title punctuation, as necessary. Be sure to place each mark of punctuation precisely.

> **Sample:**
>
> Some teenagers dream of owning their first car; however, I dream of owning a massively gigantic truck !

The guidance counselor said to me, What do you want to do after high school ?"
Well, I had my answer ready.

Im fascinated by powerful trucks, including semis and dump trucks. Even the parts of trucks interest me: for instance, a dump trucks tires can be over 12 feet high! The British have an unusual word for their largest trucks: juggernauts. I enjoy reading about huge heavy juggernauts, chunky lifesaving, fire engines and "road trains". Road trains are a long-haul method in Australia; they transport goods across the Outback.

My friends say being a truck driver would be boring; however, I disagree. Huge trucks are awe-inspiring driving; one would be fantastic. Many long-haul drivers equip their trucks with the following sleeping bunks, hot plates and small refrigerators. Ill become a truck driver; one day just watch me. Ill write a book about my life on the road One Truck Drivers Adventures . "

Fill in the puzzle by answering each question that follows. Do not use spaces between words. Choose your answers from the list below. (You can use each choice more than once.)

period question mark exclamation point comma semicolon

colon apostrophe quotation mark underlining italics

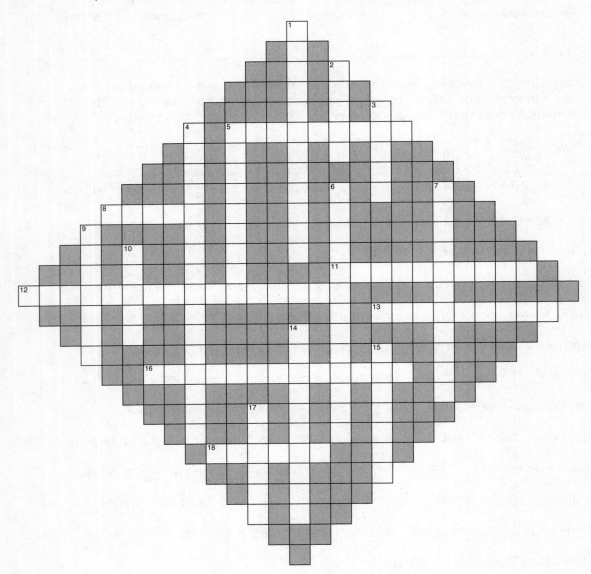

ACROSS

5. I work with *however* and a comma to join sentences. *What am I?*

8. I function as a divider between items in a list. *What am I?*

11. I show where letters got left out in a contraction. *What am I?*

DOWN

1. You should use me to end a sentence that asks a question. *What am I?*

2. Use me to draw attention to what follows. *What am I?*

3. Use two of me to set off an interrupting word group. *What am I?*

12. I am really, really good at showing strong emotion! *What am I?*

13. Use me to join two sentences without a coordinating conjunction. *What am I?*

16. I always come in pairs. *What am I?*

18. You need me to make a statement. *What am I?*

4. Use me to show that your command is urgent. *What am I?*

5. When items in a series contain commas, use me between the items. *What am I?*

6. I help you show which are a speaker's exact words. *What am I?*

7. Use me to punctuate a book title when you are writing by hand. *What am I?*

9. In printed text, I signal that a title refers to a long work. *What am I?*

10. I work with *and* or *but* to join sentences. *What am I?*

14. My job is to help words take on their possessive forms. *What am I?*

17. I belong at the end of a polite request. *What am I?*

15. BONUS QUESTION: My title should be punctuated with quotation marks. *What am I?* (Answer is not listed among the choices on page 164.)

For Activity 3, read the following poem.

An Old Story
Edwin Arlington Robinson

Strange that I did not know him then,
    That friend of mine!
I did not even show him then
    One friendly sign;

But cursed him for the ways he had
    To make me see
My envy of the praise he had
    For praising me.

I would have rid the earth of him
    Once, in my pride. . . .
I never knew the worth of him
    Until he died.

Use "An Old Story" to do each task that follows.

1. How many sentences are in this poem? _____

2. Robinson uses one semicolon in the poem. Does he follow the rules for using semicolons, or does he break the rules? Explain your answer.

   _____

   _____

   _____

3. In line 2, an exclamation point follows the words "friend of mine." However, in line 1, the speaker said, "I did not know him." How does the exclamation point help you understand what the speaker is actually saying here? (***Hint:*** Think about what kind of emotion Robinson is expressing with the exclamation point.)

   _____

   _____

   _____

   _____

4. If you could ask the narrator of this poem one question, what would it be?

   _____

   _____

Writing Application

Using Punctuation

Have you ever realized that you have underappreciated someone? What did you do after making this realization?

On a separate sheet of paper, write **two** paragraphs of at least **five** sentences describing the person you underappreciated, the reason you probably responded in this way, and what you did after you realized the person's true worth. Show off your punctuation skills by using a variety of punctuation marks and check your work for accuracy.

ACTIVITY 4

As you know, we use quotation marks to enclose a speaker's exact words. In stories, a conversation between two or more speakers is called *dialogue,* and the same rules of punctuation apply to their words.

In the following passage, insert quotation marks as needed. The two characters, Deborah and Janey, are Irish immigrants living in a poverty-stricken American mill town.

from "Life in the Iron-Mills"
Rebecca Harding Davis

While she [Deborah] was skinning the potatoes, and munching them, a noise behind her made her stop.

Janey! she called, lifting the candle and peering into the darkness. Janey, are you there?

A heap of ragged coats was heaved up, and the face of a young girl emerged, staring sleepily at the woman.

Deborah, she said, at last, I'm here the night.

Yes, child. Hur's[1] welcome, she said, quietly eating on.

The girl's face was haggard and sickly; her eyes were heavy with sleep and hunger: real Milesian[2] eyes they were, dark, delicate blue, glooming out from black shadows with a pitiful fright.

I was alone, she said, timidly.

Where's the father? asked Deborah, holding out a potato, which the girl greedily seized.

He's beyant,[3]—wid Haley,—in the stone house.[4]

---

[1] *Hur's:* She's (dialect for "You're")

[2] *Milesian*: Irish

[3] *beyant*: beyond

[4] *the stone house*: jail

Writing Application

Using Quotation Marks in Dialogue

You are hungry. You are *starving*. You are RAVENOUS! The only problem is, you have only one baked potato to eat—plain, no butter, no cheese, no "fixings." Just as you resign yourself to forcing down this drab food to ease your hunger, you notice a stranger nearby, who is just as ravenous as you. What do the two of you say to each other?

Write a dialogue of at least **ten** sentences between two people who are both ravenous. One person has one potato, and the other person has no food. Use quotation marks to punctuate the dialogue, as appropriate.

Punctuation

It's time to take a break from traditional grammar exercises. The following activities ask you to explore how people use punctuation in the real world, outside your classroom walls. Which activity sparks your interest? Choose an activity to complete; then, with your teacher's approval, share the results with your classmates. Have a good time!

And the Winner Is . . .

Which mark of punctuation gets used the most? Do a survey of printed materials of all sorts—textbooks, street signs, advertisements, newspapers, magazines, office memos, cartoon strips, and so on. Rank the marks of punctuation taught in Part Two of this book according to frequency of use and explain why you think they rank in this order.

Ain't It Fabulous?

Why do writers use contractions in some works, but not in others? Take a look at various kinds of writing—books, e-mails, office memos, job applications, newspaper articles, etc. What kinds of writing contain contractions, and what kinds do not? Is it ever okay to use the word *ain't*? Write a rule, or guideline, for when to use contractions and when, if ever, to use *ain't*. With your teacher's approval, write this rule on the chalkboard for your class.

I've a Dream!

Find a copy of a famous speech, such as Lincoln's Gettysburg Address or Martin Luther King Jr.'s "I Have a Dream." Rewrite the speech, using contractions whenever possible. Then compare the two versions. How does the writer's treatment of contractions influence the mood and force of the speech? With your teacher's approval, read or recite the speech with contractions to your class. Discuss how using contractions affected the way you spoke the sentences aloud.

If Commas Could Talk

If each punctuation mark became a person, animal, or object, what would each one be? Would the question mark be a timid child? What would the exclamation point then be? If you like to draw, create visual images of **five** punctuation marks as persons, animals, or objects. For each, write a comment spoken by that "character"—for example, the exclamation point might say, "Watch out, world! You can't hold me back!" Be sure to use correct punctuation.

¿What Did You Say?

Do you speak or study a language other than English? How does the other language use punctuation, as compared to English? For example, in written Spanish, a sentence that expresses a question begins with an upside-down question mark and ends with a right-side-up question mark. Document as many comparisons as you can—similarities and differences. Write example sentences using the punctuation in both languages.

Your Name in Print

Find a magazine, Web site, or contest that welcomes submissions from young writers. Make sure the publication is reputable. For example, Teen Ink publishes a monthly magazine, a Web site, and a book series consisting only of material written by teenagers. Write a poem or story for such a publication, and submit it! Of course, check your submission carefully for correct punctuation. (You can find Teen Ink on the Web at www.teenink.com.)

I'll Never Forget You

Remembering all the rules of comma usage can be difficult. Create an eye-catching poster that lists comma rules. For example, write each rule in a different color marker, perhaps arranged inside a giant comma. Clip bits of text from magazines that show commas being used correctly and cover the bare space on the poster with these clippings. Use your imagination!

enTITLEment

On poster board, create a visual reminder of which titles need quotation marks and which need italics/underlining. First, photocopy or cut out examples of each kind of title discussed in Lesson 22. For instance, cut the title off a magazine cover, or photocopy the title page of a book. Affix each title to the poster and label it (short story, newspaper, etc.). Then, with an ink color that stands out, add big quotation marks or underlining to each title, as appropriate.

Punctuation

Directions: Look at the item with the same number as the underlined part. Circle the letter of the best replacement for the underlined part. If the current part is best, then circle *A* or *F* for *NO CHANGE*.

For a week, <u>its</u> been raining cats and

1

_____ **1. A.** NO CHANGE

      B. it was

      C. its'

      D. it's

<u>dogs: however, some</u> kids decide to eat lunch in the

2

picnic pavilion next to the school.

_____ **2. F.** NO CHANGE

      G. dogs however, some

      H. dogs; however, some

      J. dogs, however; some

Are they <u>crazy</u>, I think so.

3

_____ **3. A.** NO CHANGE

      B. crazy.

      C. crazy?

      D. crazy!

Anyway, this group of three guys and three girls starts running toward the picnic pavilion. <u>In the sky. thunder</u>

4

crashes with a

_____ **4. F.** NO CHANGE

      G. In the sky, thunder

      H. In the sky's thunder

      J. In the sky thunder,

huge <u>KABOOM!</u> One of the girls shrieks and trips in

5

the mud.

_____ **5. A.** NO CHANGE

      B. KABOOM?

      C. KABOOM.

      D. KABOOM!"

She grabs a <u>guys</u> jacket, and they both go down. Splat!

6

Mud flies everywhere.

_____ **6. F.** NO CHANGE

      G. guys'

      H. guys's

      J. guy's

The two guys running behind them trip on the <u>couple and they</u> crash down, too.

7

_____ **7. A.** NO CHANGE

      B. couple, and they

      C. couple; and they

      D. couple: and they

The other girls start laughing their heads <u>off</u> The rain is
$\qquad$ 8
coming down in torrents, and these six people are just
standing out there, rulers of

	8.	F.	NO CHANGE
		G.	off?
		H.	off.
		J.	off,

<u>their own private universe</u>.
$\qquad$ 9

	9.	A.	NO CHANGE
		B.	they're own private universe.
		C.	their own private universe;
		D.	their' own private universe.

For some <u>reason; I wish</u> I was out there covered in
$\qquad$ 10
mud, too.

	10.	F.	NO CHANGE
		G.	reason: I wish
		H.	reason, I wish
		J.	reason? I wish

PART 2

Directions: In each item, certain parts are underlined and labeled. Circle the letter of the underlined part that contains an error. If the item has no error, circle *E* for *No error*.

_____ 11. <u>W. H. Auden</u> wrote, "<u>Some</u> books are undeservedly <u>forgotten; none</u> are
    A   **B**   **C**

    undeservedly <u>remembered</u>". <u>No error</u>
        D   **E**

_____ 12. Franz <u>Kafka, author</u> of the short novel *The Metamorphosis,* once <u>wrote,</u> "A book
      A   **B**   **C**

    ought to be an icepick to break up the frozen sea within <u>us</u>." <u>No error</u>
                   D **E**

_____ 13. "<u>There</u> is no such thing as a moral or an immoral <u>book</u>" said Oscar <u>Wilde.</u> "Books
    A   **B**   **C**

    are well written, or badly written. That is <u>all</u>." <u>No error</u>
                D **E**

_____ 14. Colette once said, "<u>When</u> one can <u>read, can</u> penetrate the enchanted realm of
         A   **B**

    <u>books</u>, why <u>write</u>"? Ironically, Colette wrote over 50 novels. <u>No error</u>
    C   **D**   **E**

_____ 15. Leon Uris had this to <u>say:</u> "To me a writer is one of the most important soldiers
          A

    in the fight for the survival of the human <u>race.</u>" "He must stay at <u>his</u> post in the
                 B   **C**

    thick of fire to serve the cause of <u>mankind</u>." <u>No error</u>
             D   **E**

3 Capitalization

English uses capital letters to set particular words apart from surrounding words. The reasons to do so are varied. For example, a capital letter marks the beginning of a sentence or direct quote. It helps set proper nouns apart from common nouns. In the following lessons, you will review these and other reasons for using capital letters as well as guidelines for using capitalization correctly.

24 Helpful Capitalization Rules

We use capital letters to draw attention to particular words for specific reasons.

 1. Capitalize the first word of a sentence.

The circus is coming to town this summer.

 2. Capitalize the first word in a quotation if the quotation is a complete sentence.

He said, "**D**o you want to get tickets to the circus?"

"**I**f you want to go," I replied, "then I'll go with you."

(In the second part of the quotation, *then* is not capitalized because it continues the complete sentence begun with *If*. Notice that no mark of end punctuation comes between *If* and *then*.)

Written dialogue often contains incomplete sentences that stand alone like sentences. In such cases, capitalize the first letter in a word or word group set as a sentence.

He said, "**R**eady to go?"

I pointed to my bare feet. "**O**ne minute."

 3. Capitalize the pronoun *I*.

Each weekday morning **I** eat fruit and oatmeal.

Maybelle and **I** installed the new software.

ACTIVITY 1

In the following passage, cross out each lowercase letter that should be capitalized and write the capital letter above it. The passage is taken from *The War of the Worlds* by H. G. Wells, a novel about Martians landing in an English village and launching an attack on humans. The first two errors are corrected for you as samples.

    W

"w̶e can't possibly stay here," I̶ said; and as i spoke the firing reopened for a moment

upon the common.[1]

"but where are we to go?" said my wife in terror.

i thought, perplexed. then i remembered her cousins at leatherhead.

"leatherhead!" i shouted above the sudden noise.

[1]*common:* open public land

she looked away from me downhill. the people were coming out of their houses, astonished.

"how are we to get to leatherhead?" she said.

Writing Application — Using Capitalization in Dialogue

Use your imagination to continue the conversation between the speaker and his wife, begun in Activity 1. What will be the speaker's idea for getting to Leatherhead, a town some distance away? What will they say about the attacking Martians? Write **eight to ten** lines of dialogue, using capitalization and quotation marks correctly. (You can review the rules for using quotation marks in dialogue in Lesson 21.)

ACTIVITY 2

Can you unscramble the words of this quotation of E. M. Forster's words? With your teacher's approval, you may choose to work with a classmate to complete this activity.

Directions: Drop the letters from each vertical column—not necessarily in the order in which they appear—into the empty boxes below them to spell words. Use each letter only once. The quotation reads from left to right, line by line. Black squares indicate spaces; periods mark the ends of sentences. Once you unscramble the quotation, write it on the lines provided, using capitalization and quotation marks correctly.

I	A	F	O	O	T	D	S	I	T	A	C	E	U	H	A	R	E	E
I	T	F	H	I	E	M	T	S	O	O	G	I	U	E	E	I	F	
	I		P	R	M	A	I		S	N	T	R	S	R	T	T	U	
	N					I					C					R		
										C								•
			O															
				L								T					•	

E. M. Forster wrote, _____

_____

_____

 4. Capitalize proper nouns, their abbreviations, and proper adjectives.

PROPER NOUNS: **M**averick **B**oulevard, **P**acific **T**rust **C**orporation

ABBREVIATIONS: **M**averick **B**lvd., **P**acific **T**rust **C**orp.

PROPER ADJECTIVES: **P**uerto **R**ican school system, **M**exican president

Proper nouns include the names of days of the week, months, and holidays.

Friday, **A**pril, **T**hanksgiving **D**ay, **L**abor **D**ay

(*Note:* The names of the seasons—spring, summer, fall/autumn, winter—are not capitalized.)

5. Capitalize titles.

Capitalize the first, last, and main words of a title. Do not capitalize *a, an, the,* and short prepositions such as *of* unless they are the first or last word of the title.

The class read *The **O**ld **M**an and the **S**ea* by Ernest Hemingway.

Alicia memorized Judie Strouf's poem "**K**enyan **T**rain."

*The **Y**oung **M**an from **A**tlanta* won the Pulitzer Prize for Drama in 1995.

6. In business and personal letters, capitalize the first word and all nouns in the *salutation*. Capitalize only the first word in the *closing*.

SALUTATION:	**D**ear **Mr. S**tetson:	**D**ear **S**ir or **M**adam:	**D**ear **A**unt **A**beni,
CLOSING:	**S**incerely,	**V**ery truly yours,	**Y**our nephew,

ACTIVITY 3

Copy the following, adding needed capitals.

> **Sample:**
>
> "a rose for emily"   "A Rose for Emily"
> (a short story)

1. dear professor chung: _____

2. sal's organic gardens, inc. _____

3. *the washington post*   _____
   (a newspaper)

4. thursday, june 3   _____

5. dear dr. champion: _____

6. 1312 hyacinth st.   _____

7. the peruvian mountains   _____

8. sincerely yours,   _____

9. "ode on a grecian urn"   _____
   (a poem)

10. your friend,   _____

Copy the following, adding needed capitals.

> **Sample:**
>
> as soon as i saw oksana, i asked, "are we still going out on friday night?"
>
> _As soon as I saw Oksana, I asked, "Are we still going out on Friday night?"_

1. "while you're at fresh foods mart," mom said, "please buy eggs."

   _____

   _____

2. "did you finish reading *the great gatsby?*" mr. connor asked.

   _____

   _____

3. the central american countries lie between north america and south america.

   _____

   _____

4. standing before the class, i recited "trees," by sergeant joyce kilmer.

   _____

   _____

5. jill glanced at me. "the time?" she said. looking at my watch, i replied, "two o'clock."

   _____

   _____

Here are some specific kinds of proper nouns that require capital letters.

Names of particular persons, real or imaginary

Rosa Parks, J. R. R. Tolkien, Sandra Day O'Connor, Sherlock Holmes, Scooby Doo

Geographical names

Wyoming, the Florida Keys, Orange County, Seattle, the Everglades

Titles of organizations, companies, and buildings

Lions Club, Public Broadcast Company, Sears Tower

Political parties, nations, governmental bodies

Democratic Party, Republican Party, Congress, Department of the Interior

Titles of persons showing office, rank, profession

President Lincoln, General Marshall, Dr. Koop, Judge Rogers

Using Titles

In some languages, the word *the* is commonly used before a title, as in *Where is the Professor Jimenez?* In English, however, *the* is not used before a title.

EXAMPLES: Where is Professor Jimenez. (NOT *the Professor Jimenez*)

I report to General Marshall. (NOT *the General Marshall*)

There are two exceptions to this rule. In English, we often use *the* before the titles *Reverend* and *Honorable.*

EXAMPLES: Where is the Honorable Judge Rogers?

Our wedding was performed by the Reverend Jenkins.

Names of planets, satellites, stars, and constellations

Jupiter, **G**anymede, **S**irius, the **B**ig **D**ipper

The words *sun* and *moon* are not capitalized except as the first word in a sentence. The word *earth* is capitalized only when discussed as a specific planet.

Much of the earth is covered in water.

The three planets nearest the sun are **M**ercury, **V**enus, and **E**arth.

Brand names

Campbell's soups, **N**abisco cookies, **K**leenex tissues, **G**reen **G**iant peas

Names referring to God, holy books, religions

the **A**lmighty, the **H**oly **B**ible, the book of **G**enesis, the **K**oran, **J**udaism, **H**induism

ACTIVITY 5

Write an answer to each question on the line provided, using capitals as needed.

Samples:

a. Name a constellation. __Little Dipper__

b. Name a club you would enjoy joining. __Journalism Club__

1. Who is the U.S. president right now? _____

2. What is this president's political party? _____

3. What brand of snacks do you prefer? _____

4. What person from history would you like to meet? _____

5. Which planet (besides Earth and the moon) interests you most? _____

6. In what state do you live? _____

7. In what state or country would you like to vacation? _____

8. What is your favorite cartoon character? _____

9. What is your English teacher's name, including his or her title? _____

10. What is the name of your school? _____

Certain items require extra thought if you are to capitalize them correctly.

Sections of the country

the **S**outheast, the **N**orthwest, the **S**outhwest

The ***Southwest*** is known for its hot, dry climate.

Do not capitalize these names if they are merely compass points.

Iowa is ***northeast*** of Kansas.

Family relationships

Capitalize words used as a name or used before a name in direct address.

Dad, **M**other, **A**unt **P**etunia, **G**randpa, **C**ousin **S**teven

Happy birthday, ***Mother!***

Do not capitalize *mom, dad,* or titles such as *aunt* following a possessive pronoun.

*My **dad*** and *my **aunt Penelope*** grew up in Arkansas.

*Their **grandpa*** was born in Tennessee.

School subjects: languages and numbered courses

Capitalize the names of language courses: ***French, English, German, Spanish***

Capitalize the names of numbered courses: ***Algebra 2, Mathematics 4, Art 3***

Do not capitalize the names of unnumbered courses, except for languages: *history, advanced chemistry, world cultures, biology, Italian*

ACTIVITY 6 _____

Circle the letter of the item that uses capitalization correctly.

Samples:

a. 1. Have you ever visited the south?

2. Have you ever visited the South?

b. 1. Does Aseem's dad own the fish market on Fifth Street?

2. Does Aseem's Dad own the fish market on Fifth Street?

1. **a.** our uncle Will

   b. our Uncle Will

2. **a.** History class

   b. history class

3. **a.** travel to the northwest

   b. travel to the Northwest

4. **a.** Hello, Cousin Ziggy.

   b. Hello, cousin Ziggy.

5. **a.** my german homework

   b. my German homework

6. **a.** a gift from Grandma

   b. a gift from grandma

7. **a.** May I go, mom?

   b. May I go, Mom?

8. **a.** southeast of Bismarck

   b. Southeast of Bismarck

9. **a.** Chemistry 101

   b. chemistry 101

10. **a.** my father

    b. my Father

25 Review of Capitalization

Capitalize

- the first word in a sentence
- the first word in a direct quotation that is a complete sentence
- the pronoun *I*
- proper nouns, their abbreviations, and proper adjectives
- the first and all main words in titles
- the first word and all nouns in a salutation, and the first word in a closing

ACTIVITY 1

In the following short story and its title, cross out each lowercase letter that should be capitalized and write the capital letter above it. The first sentence is completed for you as a sample. (Don't forget to correct the title!)

movie night with my closest friends

"W̶ho wants popcorn?" sang out J̶essica, plunking a white plastic bowl on the coffee

table. buttery puffs of pop secret popcorn sloshed out. "whoops!" she squealed.

"none for me," said aidan, "but i'll eat your pizza for you." grinning, he reached for jessi-

ca's paper plate, already soaked with sausage grease. pizza from south side deli was the

best: real mediterranean-style pizza, not that generic american kind.

jessica slapped his hand, squealing, "keep your sticky fingers away, mr. galloway!" she

batted her eyelashes, no doubt feeling clever for addressing aidan by his surname.

i rolled my eyes. waving the copy of *pirates of the caribbean,* i said, "let's get this show

on the road."

jessica and aidan looked at me with startled expressions. i'm not kidding—i think they

just realized i was there too. sheesh!

"catch you later," i called, grabbing my pizza and the movie. jessica's front door clicked

shut behind me.

Writing Application — Using Capital Letters

Have you ever felt invisible among friends? Or, on the flip side, have you ever gotten so focused on one particular person that everyone else seemed invisible?

On a separate sheet of paper, write a short narrative (similar in length to the one in Activity 1) about one of these scenarios. Use the first-person point of view (use *I*, like the story above does) and include dialogue. Check your work for proper capitalization.

Decide whether each item is capitalized correctly or incorrectly. If it is correct, write
correct **on the line provided. If it is incorrect, write the item correctly.**

Samples:

a. the novel *a Wrinkle in time* _____ the novel A Wrinkle in Time _____

b. I said, "Who's there?" _____ correct _____

1. on Valentine's day _____

2. Dear Ms. Layton: _____

3. last autumn _____

4. my Sister _____

5. next saturday _____

6. the moon _____

7. Department Of The Treasury _____

8. a trip to the Northeast _____

9. yellowstone national park _____

10. Thank you, Uncle Wally. _____

11. our history class _____

12. ozarka bottled water _____

13. on Parker ave. _____

14. the planet venus _____

15. Ford motor co. _____

16. bart simpson _____

17. Hello, mayor Wilson. _____

18. the senate _____

19. a test in government IV _____

20. a country in Europe _____

For Activity 3, read the following poem.

When I Heard the Learn'd Astronomer
Walt Whitman

When I heard the learn'd astronomer,

When the proofs, the figures, were ranged in columns before me,

When I was shown the charts and diagrams, to add, divide, and measure them,

When I, sitting, heard the astronomer where he lectured with much applause in the lecture-room,

How soon unaccountable I became tired and sick,

Till rising and gliding out I wander'd off by myself,

In the mystical moist night-air, and from time to time,

Look'd up in perfect silence at the stars.

ACTIVITY 3 _____

Use "When I Heard the Learn'd Astronomer" to answer the following questions. Except for item 1, write your answers in complete sentences.

1. How many sentences make up this poem? _____

2. To answer question 1, which was more useful—studying the poem's capital letters, or studying its punctuation?

   _____

   _____

   _____

3. How does Whitman break the rules of capitalization you learned in Lesson 24?

   _____

   _____

4. What seems to be Whitman's logic for using capital letters?

   _____

5. Based on your knowledge of poetry, how common is it for poets to use capitalization as Whitman has?

   _____

6. Based on your answers to questions 3, 4, and 5, above, write a new capitalization rule to address the needs of poetry.

   _____

   _____

Capitalization

It's time to take a break from traditional grammar exercises. The following activities ask you to explore how people use capitalization in the real world, outside your classroom walls. Which activity sparks your interest? Choose an activity to complete; then, with your teacher's approval, share the results with your classmates. Have a good time!

"Love looks not with the eyes, but with the mind"

Everyone loves a pithy saying. Collect a batch of your favorite quotations—from literature, music, interviews, wherever. Type up a page of these quotations, using punctuation and capital letters as needed. Be sure to note the source of each quote. (The quotation above, by the way, comes from Shakespeare's *A Midsummer Night's Dream,* Act I, Scene 1, line 234.)

IMHO

If you exchange e-mails or text messages with friends, chances are you know what IMHO means: It is a kind of shorthand for "in my humble opinion." The same goes for FYI (for your information) and BTW (by the way). How many of these shorthand phrases can you list and explain? Include any original ones you and your friends have created. Write a guideline explaining when it is acceptable to use these shorthand phrases and when the writer should spell out complete words.

Harmonize While You Capitalize

If you are rhythmically inclined, write a song, rap, or rhyme that will help people remember the rules of capitalization. Share your creation with your classmates.

DO NOT ENTER

"Environmental print" includes all the words you read as you go about your daily life. It includes the milk carton and cereal box, traffic signs, store signs, billboards, bumper stickers, the sides of buses—the list goes on. How does environmental print use capital letters? Do a survey and summarize your findings. Include specific examples with explanations of why each uses capitalization the way it does.

Breaking the Rules

T. S. Eliot advised, "It's not wise to violate the rules until you know how to observe them." Collect examples of broken capitalization rules from e-mails, advertisements, store circulars, etc. For each example, write why the writer probably broke the rule and whether the result is effective. Some writers break rules from carelessness or ignorance; don't hesitate to analyze these examples, too.

Fly Me to the Moon

What better place to explore capital letters than a vacation brochure? These fun texts are chock-full of geographical names, hotel and company names, months, days, nations, holidays, proper adjectives, and so on. Choose a destination that interests you and write a vacation brochure to lure visitors there. Who knows, maybe you'll be a travel writer one day.

<H1>Welcome Page</H1>

Are capital letters important to computer programming? Enlighten the uninitiated. Create a simple Web page or write a few lines of code to show your classmates and explain how you used capital and/or lowercase letters to achieve the desired results.

Sie ist Studentin

How do the rules for capitalization work in other languages? For example, in the German sentence *Sie ist Studentin* (She is a student), the noun *Studentin* is capitalized. In the English translation, however, *student* is not capitalized. German uses capitalization differently from English. Compare English usage of capitalization to that of another language. Include examples in each language.

Capitalization

PART 1

Directions: On the numbered lines, write the best correction for each numbered, underlined part. If the underlined part needs no change, write *no error*.

november 29, 2004
1

Mega movies
2

408 S. century st.
3

Hollywood, CA 91601
4

dear Ms. Biancavilla:
5

Thank you for your assistance during our tele-
6
phone conversation on friday, November 26,
7
2004. As I mentioned, I bought two movie DVDs

from mega movies to give as christmas pres-
8   9
ents. They are *Never been Kissed* and *under*
10
the Tuscan Sun. When the movies arrived in the
11
mail, they had been run over by a Truck. The
12
black tire marks are clearly visible on the pack-

aging, which i'm enclosing, along with the dam-
13
aged movies.

I am eager to receive the replacement copies,
which you promised to send immediately; thank
you very much.   14

Very truly yours,
15
Caitlyn Flores

1. _____

2. _____

3. _____

4. _____

5. _____

6. _____

7. _____

8. _____

9. _____

10. _____

11. _____

12. _____

13. _____

14. _____

15. _____

Directions: Each item contains at least one error in capitalization. Circle the word or words with errors. Then, on the lines provided, rewrite the word or words, adding capital letters as needed.

16. Mom's shopping list included ore ida frozen French fries.

_____

17. Our city's department of parks and recreation put out maps of all the parks.

_____

18. Ty's report is on president John F. Kennedy and the cuban missile crisis.

_____

19. We always send grandmother a gift on mother's day.

_____

20. What did you think of professor Preston's midterm in political science 1311?

_____

21. The library has copies of the torah, the koran, the Bible, and other religious writings.

_____

22. Wendy said that we are going to joe pool lake for the sophomore class picnic.

_____

23. suddenly a baseball came out of nowhere, smacked my nose, and broke it.

_____

24. Can you locate perseus and orion in the night sky?

_____

25. The Czechoslovakian playwright Vaclav havel wrote *the Garden Party*.

PART 2

_____

Spelling

Along with using proper punctuation and capitalization, spelling words correctly is crucial to communicating well. The following lessons offer helpful spelling rules and give guidelines for spelling plural nouns. Starting right now, you can become a better speller.

26 Helpful Spelling Rules

The following simple rules can help you to spell a great many words correctly.

---

1. Writing *ie* and *ei.*

Write *i* before *e* except after *c*, or when sounded like *a* as in *neighbor* and *weigh*.

i before **e**:	niece, chief, field, believe
except after **c**:	conceit, receive, ceiling, deceit, perceive, receipt
sounded like **a**:	eight, sleigh, freight, veil, reign
Exceptions:	efficient, science, neither, protein, caffeine, weird

---

ACTIVITY 1

Fill in the missing letters. Then, write the complete word at the right.

Sample:

You can **ach**___*ie*___**ve** your dreams.   _____*achieve*_____

1. Yes, I have **exper**_____**nce** in retail sales.   _____

2. Blood flows in your **v**_____**ns**.   _____

3. **Br**_____**fly**, he outlined the plan.   _____

4. Show your **rec**_____**pt** for refunds.   _____

5. Did you like _____**ther** song?   _____

6. Roy guided the horse with **r**_____**ns**.   _____

7. Do you **bel**_____**ve** me?   _____

8. The graduates moved **th**_____**r** tassels.   _____

9. Coffee contains a lot of **caff**_____**ne**.   _____

10. Stop, **th**_____**f**!   _____

---

2. Adding prefixes.

When adding a prefix, do not change the spelling of the original word.

unpack, **un**natural, **dis**ability, **il**legal, **mis**fortune

---

ACTIVITY 2

Combine each prefix in the first box with a word in the second box. Write the new word in the third box. (Some words in Box 2 will be left unused.) You may choose to ask your teacher's approval to use a dictionary. One word is created for you as a sample.

Box 1		Box 2		Box 3
co		happy		**1.** tricycle
dis		sense		**2.**
en		operate		**3.**
in		force		**4.**
non		wind		**5.**
pre		fiction		**6.**
re		view		**7.**
super	+	angle	=	**8.**
tri		tie		**9.**
un		courage		**10.**
		corporate		**11.**
		turn		
		honest		
		natural		
		correct		
		cycle		

---

 3. Words ending in silent *e*.

(a) Drop the *e* to add a suffix beginning with a vowel.

erase̷able, compet̷eing, jok̷eer, cut̷eest, argu̷eing

Exceptions: mil**e**age, dy**e**ing

(b) Keep the *e* to add a suffix beginning with a consonant.

hat**e**ful, sol**e**ly, saf**e**ty, amaz**e**ment, hop**e**ful

Exceptions: truly, ninth, wholly, argument, judgment, awful

ACTIVITY 3

Add the suffix to the base word in parentheses and write the new word on the blank.

Samples:

a. I am _____enclosing_____ my résumé. *(enclose + ing)*

b. That gadget surely is _____useful_____. *(use + ful)*

1. The detective will take your _____ now. *(state + ment)*

2. This town has a _____ of vegetarian restaurants. *(scarce + ity)*

3. Is the disease _____? *(cure + able)*

4. I am _____ happy for you! *(true + ly)*

5. The firefighters' efforts were _____. *(courage + ous)*

6. All _____ standards have been met or exceeded. *(safe + ty)*

7. Telling the truth tactfully is always _____. *(admire + able)*

8. That woman with the net is _____ butterflies. *(chase + ing)*

9. Did you make _____ for a babysitter? *(arrange + ments)*

10. Katrina, a textile artist, is _____ the cloth with red dye. *(dye + ing)*

---

 4. Words ending in *y*.

(a) When the word ends in a <u>vowel and *y*</u>, keep the *y* when adding a suffix

enjo**y**ment, pla**y**ing, bu**y**er, betra**y**al, jo**y**ous

Exceptions: day + ly = daily   pay + ed = paid   *(y changed to i)*

(b) When the word ends in a <u>consonant and *y*</u>, change the *y* to *i* before a suffix not beginning with *i*.

fun**ny** + er = funnier   plen**ty** + ful = plentiful   sil**ly** + ness = silliness

Exceptions: shy + er = shyer   dry + ly = dryly   carry + ing = carrying

---

ACTIVITY 4

Add the suffix to the base word in parentheses, and use the new word in a sentence.

Samples:

a. *(convey + ed)*   _____The merchandise was conveyed by truck._____

b. *(apply + ed)*   _____Chris applied glue to the airplane's wing._____

1. *(boy + ish)* _____

2. *(say + ing)* _____

3. *(noisy + er)* _____

4. *(day + ly)* _____

5. *(bully + ing)* _____

6. *(survey + or)* _____

7. *(easy + ly)* _____

8. *(play + ful)* _____

9. *(buoy + ant)* _____

10. *(library + an)* _____

---

5. Adding *ly* or *ness*.

When adding *ly* or *ness*, do not change the spelling of the original word.

loud**ly**, famous**ly**, beautiful**ly**, thin**ness**, handsome**ness**

Note: When adding **ly** or **ness** to a word ending in **y**, follow the rule for words ending in **y** (rule 4, on page 192).

angr**y** + ly = angr**i**ly   tard**y** + ness = tard**i**ness   sill**y** + ness = sill**i**ness

---

ACTIVITY 5 _____

Add either *ly* or *ness* to ten of the following words, and use each new word in a sentence.

casual	homeless	grateful	near	clean	angry
rare	crazy	exact	conscious	cheerful	love

Samples:

a. *Derek consciously ate very, very slowly.*

b. *The casualness of her lie surprised me.*

1. _____

2. _____

3. _____

4. _____

5. _____

6. _____

7. _____

8. _____

9. _____

10. _____

---

6. Doubling a final consonant before a suffix beginning with a vowel.

(a) Double the consonant if the word is one syllable or the accent is on the final syllable.

batter, bi**gg**est, forgo**tt**en, prope**ll**ed, admi**tt**ed

(b) Do not double the consonant if it is preceded by more than one vowel.

clea**n**ing, sai**l**ed, drea**m**er, foo**l**ish, revie**w**er

---

ACTIVITY 6

Add the suffix to each word, as indicated, and write the new word on the line provided.

Samples:

a. big + er = _____bigger_____   **b.** foam + ing = _____foaming_____

1. flat + est = _____   **9.** squeal + ing = _____

2. zip + er   = _____   **10.** pot + er   = _____

3. leap + ing = _____   **11.** expel + ed = _____

4. stoop + ed = _____   **12.** benefit + ed = _____

5. snap + y = _____   **13.** patrol + ing = _____

6. stop + ed = _____   **14.** deter + ent = _____

7. freak + ish = _____   **15.** drop + ing = _____

8. rot + en = _____   **16.** commit + ed = _____

---

17. reveal + ing   = _____

18. appear + ance = _____

19. format + ed = _____

20. refer + ence = _____

✎ Writing
Application

Doubling (or Not Doubling)
Final Consonants

Choose **five** of the 20 base words in Activity 6, and to each one add a suffix other than the one in the activity. For example, you could add *est* to *big* to form *biggest.* On a separate sheet of paper, use each new word in a sentence.

Composition Hint

Any time you are unsure of the spelling of a word, look it up in a dictionary. Try to find it listed in each of the ways you think it is spelled. When you find it listed, you know you've found the correct spelling. However, be sure to read the definition(s) to make sure the word has the meaning you think it does. Some dictionaries are available online, or as software you can load onto your computer. Here is a sample dictionary entry for the word *effect.*

   effect *(n.)* **1.** something that follows a cause; **2.** influence; **3.** *(plural)* goods; moveable property. *(v.)* **4.** to cause to come into being; **5.** to bring about, often by surmounting obstacles.

ACTIVITY 7

Correct each of these misspellings by writing the correct spelling on the line provided. Then circle the correct spelling in the puzzle. Words may read forward, backward, up, down, or diagonally.

Words That Have to Do With Film and Theater

1. theator   _____

2. acter   _____

3. charater   _____

4. scrippt   _____

5. camra   _____

6. staig   _____

7. rehursul   _____

8. premeire   _____

9. audeince   _____

10. improvization   _____

11. costums   _____

12. desiner   _____

13. dramma   _____

14. comedie   _____

15. blokbustor   _____

16. makup   _____

17. voicover _____ **19.** cinnema _____

18. musiccal _____ **20.** screanwritor _____

```
K                               R
D T                         O   E
U B H                   T   C   H
R U S E R             V C S G   E
E K I C A Z F     J H A H N L   A
T F N O I T A S I V O R P M I   R
S T A         E M L B       D P S
U G E         S R Y E         V R A
B S C R E E N W R I T E R E E L
K T N S A U G R H V Y O M K M A
C W E G T Y D E M O C U C X I M
O I I N R A J V X I T W G T E A
L F D U O V G O R S K B P P R R
B X U A M N Q E O T U I J V E D
D M A K E U P C H A R A C T E R
Q E   N C H S I M C O Z N   D U
A L S     W K O S K G     L S A
T R M I     R V E L     A R M W
  H E J G     I B     C Z E Q
    O M Z N A       F I M N I
      T A L E P C S P I D
        C Y R U A C
          M E
```

27 Plural Nouns

Nouns have a *singular* form and a *plural* form.

 The *singular* is the form that means *only one*.

   desk, cloud, paycheck, fork, friend, etc.

 The *plural* is the form that means *more than one*.

   desks, clouds, paychecks, forks, friends, etc.

ACTIVITY 1

Write the form indicated.

> **Samples:**
>
> **a.** the plural of *textbook* _____textbooks_____
>
> **b.** the singular of *baseballs* _____baseball_____

1. the singular of *backpacks* _____

2. the plural of *hallway* _____

3. the singular of *sharks* _____

4. the plural of *computer* _____

5. the plural of *holiday* _____

Here are the singular and plural forms of a few more nouns.

SINGULAR	PLURAL
(only one)	(more than one)
song	songs
bush	bushes
wolf	wolves
mouse	mice

From the above examples, you can see that there is no single rule for forming the plurals of nouns; there are several. With the following helpful rules, you will be well on your way to spelling plurals correctly.

Rule 1. For most nouns:

Add *s* to the singular to form the plural.

SINGULAR	PLURAL
heart	hearts
bottle	bottles
cake	cakes
river	rivers

ACTIVITY 2

Make the following nouns plural.

Sample:

highway _____highways_____

1. summer _____

2. telephone _____

3. soup _____

4. classmate _____

5. town _____

6. sunset _____

7. pillow _____

8. talent _____

9. cookie _____

10. mistake _____

QUESTION: Can I form the plural of words like *class* or *dish* just by adding *s*?

ANSWER: No, because *classs* and *dishs* would be hard to pronounce. We must do something else. This brings us to Rule 2.

 Rule 2. For nouns ending in *s, sh, ch,* or *x*:

Add *es* to form the plural.

NOUNS ENDING IN *s*:   glass + es = glasses

kiss + es = kisses

NOUNS ENDING IN *sh*:	crash + es = crashes
	wish + es = wishes
NOUNS ENDING IN *ch*:	lunch + es = lunches
	crutch + es = crutches
NOUNS ENDING IN *x*:	box + es = boxes
	tax + es = taxes

ACTIVITY 3

Make the following nouns plural.

> **Samples:**
>
> **a.** ash   _ashes_
>
> **b.** church   _churches_

1. fox   _____

2. cross   _____

3. dish   _____

4. bus   _____

5. annex   _____

6. mix   _____

7. flash   _____

8. bench   _____

9. batch   _____

10. dress   _____

ACTIVITY 4

Make the following nouns plural. Some nouns require *s*, and others require *es*.

> **Samples:**
>
> **a.** seagull   _seagulls_
>
> **b.** latch   _latches_

1. genius   _____

2. elevator   _____

3. phase   _____

4. branch   _____

5. ambush   _____

6. eye   _____

7. duplex   _____

8. kitchen   _____

9. grass   _____

10. duckling   _____

 Rule 3. For most nouns ending in *f*:

Change *f* to *v* and add *es* to form the plural.

leaf	leaves
loaf	loaves
half	halves
wolf	wolves

But not in a name:

Ms. Wolf	the Wolfs

Exceptions: For some nouns ending in *f*, add *s* to form the plural.

roof	roofs
belief	beliefs
proof	proofs

Rule 4. For three nouns ending in *fe—knife, life, wife*:

Change *f* to *v* and add *s* to form the plural.

knife	knives
life	lives
wife	wives

ACTIVITY 5

Make each of the following nouns plural.

Samples:

a. grief _____griefs_____

b. shelf _____shelves_____

1. brief _____

2. life _____

3. chief _____

4. reef _____

5. self _____

6. staff _____

7. gulf _____

8. thief _____

9. calf _____

10. wife _____

ACTIVITY 6

Make each of the following nouns singular.

Samples:

a. creases _____crease_____

b. elves _____elf_____

1. sandwiches _____

2. taxes _____

3. knifes _____

4. houses _____

5. trenches _____

6. cliffs _____

7. printers _____

8. giraffes _____

9. hooves _____

10. glasses _____

Rule 5. For nouns ending in *y*:

(a) If the letter before *y* is a vowel *(a, e, i, o, u)*, add *s* to form the plural.

toy	toys
way	ways
guy	guys

(b) If the letter before *y* is a consonant, change the *y* to *i* and add *es.*

cry	cries
theory	theories
lady	ladies

ACTIVITY 7

Make each of the following nouns plural.

Samples:

a. delay _____*delays*_____

b. mystery _____*mysteries*_____

1. city _____

2. joy _____

3. way _____

4. strawberry _____

5. lullaby _____

6. fly _____

7. decoy _____

8. Saturday _____

9. cherry _____

10. January _____

Rule 6. For nouns ending in *o*:

Add *s* in most cases.

patio	patios
rodeo	rodeos
ratio	ratios
piano	pianos
auto	autos
two	twos

Exceptions: Add *es* to the following nouns:

echo	echoes
hero	heroes
potato	potatoes
tomato	tomatoes
veto	vetoes

ACTIVITY 8

Make each of the following nouns plural.

> **Samples:**
> **a.** trio _____trios_____
> **b.** hero _____heroes_____

1. cameo _____

2. echo _____

3. kangaroo _____

4. soprano _____

5. barrio _____

6. taco _____

7. radio _____

8. portfolio _____

9. volcano _____

10. potato _____

Rule 7.   Some nouns form their plurals irregularly.

SINGULAR		PLURAL	
child	mouse	children	mice
crisis	ox	crises	oxen
datum	parenthesis	data	parentheses
deer	series	deer	series
foot	shrimp	feet	shrimp
goose	syllabus	geese	syllabi
louse	thesis	lice	theses
man	tooth	men	teeth
medium	woman	media	women
moose		moose	

ACTIVITY 9

Write the form indicated.

> **Samples:**
>
> **a.** the plural of *goose*   _____geese_____
>
> **b.** the singular of *women*   _____woman_____

1. the singular of *teeth*   _____

2. the plural of *moose*   _____

3. the singular of *children*   _____

4. the plural of *foot*   _____

5. the singular of *oxen*   _____

6. the plural of *mouse*   _____

7. the singular of *men*   _____

8. the plural of *louse*   _____

9. the singular of *parentheses*   _____

10. the plural of *deer*   _____

Composition Hint

As you know from Lesson 20, the apostrophe is used to form a possessive or to make a contraction. Do not use an apostrophe to make words plural.

INSTEAD OF: *Student's* should clear their own *table's.*

WRITE: *Students* should clear their own *tables.*

ACTIVITY 10

On the line provided, write whether each underlined noun is *plural* or *possessive*.

Samples:

a. the <u>girls'</u> party   _____ possessive _____

b. <u>crates</u> of eggs   _____ plural _____

1. many funny <u>clowns</u>   _____

2. the <u>dress's</u> hem   _____

3. our <u>clients'</u> wishes   _____

4. <u>essays</u> about history   _____

5. <u>stamp's</u> design   _____

Writing Application
Using Plural and Possessive Nouns

Use each of the following nouns in a sentence. Write your sentences on a separate sheet of paper.

friends'	teachers	books	photo's	customers'
candles	e-mail's	women's	teams	seniors

For each bubble, use the hint to unscramble the letters to spell a plural noun. Write the letters of the noun in the correct order in the little boxes. One item is completed as a sample.

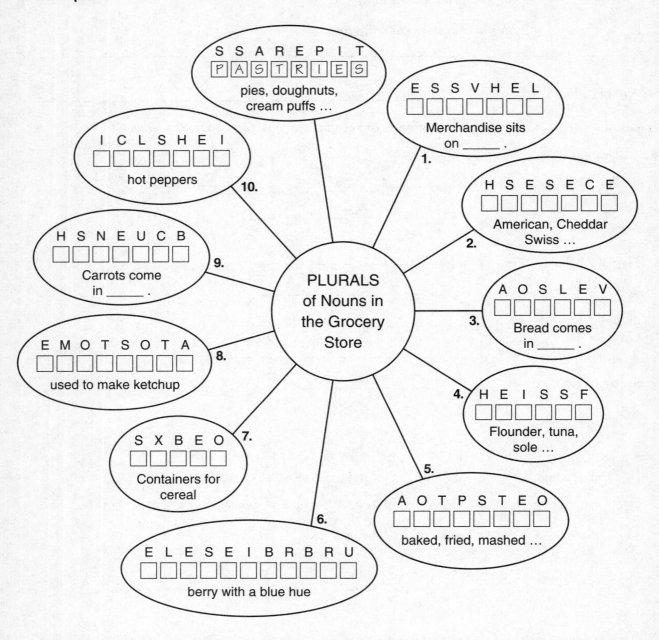

S S A R E P I T
P A S T R I E S
pies, doughnuts,
cream puffs …

E S S V H E L
Merchandise sits
on _____ .
1.

I C L S H E I
hot peppers
10.

H S E S E C E
American, Cheddar
Swiss …
2.

H S N E U C B
Carrots come
in _____ .
9.

A O S L E V
Bread comes
in _____ .
3.

E M O T S O T A
used to make ketchup
8.

4. H E I S S F
Flounder, tuna,
sole …

S X B E O
Containers for
cereal
7.

5.
A O T P S T E O
baked, fried, mashed …

6.
E L E S E I B R R B R U
berry with a blue hue

PLURALS
of Nouns in
the Grocery
Store

Writing Application

Using Plural Nouns

On a separate sheet of paper, write **ten** sentences using plural nouns. In each sentence, use **one** plural noun from the puzzle in Activity 11, along with **one** plural noun you come up with yourself. For example, a sentence using *pastries* may read something like this: *Flaky pastries were displayed inside polished glass cases.*

28 Review of Spelling

- Many words are spelled according to established rules.
- Most plurals are spelled according to established rules.
- Except on tests, you can almost always consult a dictionary to find the correct spelling of a word. Take advantage of this helpful reference source!

ACTIVITY 1

In each sentence in the following passage, underline the correct spelling of the word in parentheses.

> **Sample:**
>
> Sometimes, fact is (*truely, truly*) stranger than fiction.

(*Terrifying, Terrifieing*) dragons that feast on human beings are fiction, right? Not (*exactely, exactly*). (*Wieghing, Weighing*) up to 300 pounds, the Komodo dragon of Indonesia has been known to chase down and attack people—and eat them. Such (*viciousness, vicioussness*) is directed at its own kind, too. (*Occasionally, Occasionaly*), Komodo dragons devour each other. Newly hatched (*babys, babies*), measuring about 18 inches, live in trees for several months. Perhaps this (*unusual, unnusual*) nursery provides safety from hungry adults.

The dragon's teeth are (*certainly, certainely*) dangerous. However, the dragon's filthy mouth can cause death (*indirectly, inndirectly*). Its mouth is filled with (*microorganisms, microrganisms*). Also called germs, these microscopic creatures cause infection in the dragon's (*biten, bitten*) prey. Even if the bite doesn't kill, the infection can, (*producing, produceing*) the dragon's favorite meal—dead flesh.

The Komodo dragon is an (*amazeing, amazing*) reptile. Technically, however, it is a lizard, not a (*biologycal, biological*) dragon. It can grow up to 10 feet long, (*living, liveing*) 100 years.

Make each of the following nouns plural.

> **Samples:**
>
> **a.** zoo _____ zoos _____
>
> **b.** cherry _____ cherries _____

1. canary _____

2. torpedo _____

3. life _____

4. goose _____

5. brush _____

6. roof _____

7. speaker _____

8. crutch _____

9. annex _____

10. leaf _____

Write the form indicated.

> **Samples:**
>
> **a.** the plural of *taco* _____ tacos _____
>
> **b.** the singular of *histories* _____ history _____

1. the singular of *delays* _____

2. the plural of *rodeo* _____

3. the singular of *mysteries* _____

4. the plural of *half* _____

5. the singular of *crutches* _____

6. the plural of *tuba* _____

7. the singular of *women* _____

8. the plural of *child* _____

9. the singular of *theories* _____

10. the plural of *proof* _____

ACTIVITY 4 _____

Decide whether the underlined word is the correct spelling of the plural. If it is correct, write *correct* on the line. If it is incorrect, write the correct spelling.

> **Samples:**
>
> **a.** These <u>bag's</u> of groceries are heavy.   _____*bags*_____
>
> **b.** Along the bank, <u>canoes</u> were lined up.   _____*correct*_____

1. My old team <u>jerseys</u> are faded. _____

2. <u>Shopper's</u> crowded the aisles. _____

3. All <u>applicants'</u> were interviewed. _____

4. Several <u>paths</u> led through the forest. _____

5. What is making those <u>screeches</u>? _____

6. All <u>driver's</u> must pass the test. _____

7. Several <u>beach's</u> are near here. _____

8. Warm <u>cookie's</u> are delicious. _____

9. Are these <u>addresses</u> correct? _____

10. <u>Avocado's</u> are a tasty green fruit. _____

ACTIVITY 5 _____

Fill in the missing letters, either *ie* or *ei*. Then write the completed word at the right.

> **Sample:**
>
> a **bel**___*ie*___**f** in honesty   _____*belief*_____

1. a **f_____ld** of wheat   _____

2. the king's **r_____gn**   _____

3. to **rec_____ve** a gift   _____

4. a **qu_____t** library   _____

5. horse-drawn **sl_____gh**   _____

ACTIVITY 6 _____

Add the prefix or suffix to the word, as indicated, and write the new word on the line provided.

Samples:

a. dis + service = _____*disservice*_____

b. loose + en = _____*loosen*_____

1. theory + ize = _____

2. grate + ful = _____

3. amazing + ly = _____

4. ultra + modern = _____

5. forgot + en = _____

6. care + less = _____

7. fool + ish = _____

8. in + definite = _____

9. commit + ed = _____

10. remote + ness = _____

Spelling

It's time to take a break from traditional grammar exercises. The following activities ask you to explore how people use spelling in the real world, outside your classroom walls. Which activity sparks your interest? Choose an activity to complete; then, with your teacher's approval, share the results with your classmates. Have a good time!

Mnemonic Power

Create mnemonic devices to help people remember the spellings of tricky words. (*Mnemonic,* which begins with a silent *m,* means "assisting memory.") For example, "A principal is your PAL" helps you remember the difference between *principal* and *principle*. "**D**an **E**ats **S**trawberry **S**hortcake **E**very **R**ainy **T**uesday" helps you remember to put two *s*'s in *dessert*.

Ashley, Ashlee, or Ashleigh?

When it comes to spelling the names of people, it seems that consistency flies right out the window. Make a list of the first names of everyone in your class. Then list one or more alternate spellings for each person's name. If you could create one or two rules to govern the spelling of names, what would they be?

Word Search

Survey your classmates and compile a list of 20 difficult words to spell. Then create a word-search puzzle using these words. Using graph paper, outline a rectangle of about 15 by 20 squares. Insert letters to spell words frontward, backward, up, down, and diagonally. Use a different color pencil to fill in the remainder of the puzzle with random letters. Then, on fresh paper, create the actual puzzle using black ink and list the words to find along the side. Use your original copy to make the solution key.

A Spell Book

Every word in the English language is formed from some combination of the same 26 letters—the key is knowing how to combine the letters. Make your own "spell book" that tells how to spell words. Use a small blank notebook, or fold paper into a handmade booklet, or use a color printer. On the pages, write spelling rules and guidelines for making nouns plural. Give examples (and exceptions) for each rule. This little spell book can serve you well throughout school and beyond, so make it special, with colored ink or sketches or lists of your own most difficult words to spell.

Silent Agony

Many English words have silent letters that can make spelling the words an agony. Other letters such as *g* and *c* are pronounced differently in different words (compare *germ* and *game, cat* and *face*). What about other languages? Do you know of a language that has silent letters or letters that vary in pronunciation? Or how about a language that has virtually no silent letters? Compare the ease (or difficulty!) of spelling in English to spelling in another language. List spelling rules for each language, including examples.

Pore Spellirs Need Knot Applie

Compile a list of career opportunities, with job descriptions, for good spellers. A position as a proofreader is the tip of the iceberg.

Whose Idea Was This, Anyway?

When was the first English dictionary made? Who made it, and why? How did it affect written English, not only in its compiler's lifetime but also in the years that followed? Research the history of dictionaries in English and find the answers to these and other questions you have.

Typos

A "typo" is a typographical error. Many misspelled words in print are typos—the typist knew the correct spelling but hit a wrong key, for example. Or someone accepted a computer spell-checker's suggestion without realizing the "correction" was a different word entirely. Other printed misspellings are the result of poor spellers. Collect examples of misspelled words in print and form a poster or collage of them. What kinds of sources are most likely to contain typos and/or misspellings?

Spelling

Directions: Circle the letter of the best correction for the underlined word. If the word is already spelled correctly, circle *D* or *J* for *no error.*

_____ **1.** The first Africans arrived in the British <u>colonys</u> of North America in 1619.

    A. colonies

    B. colonyies

    C. colonyes

    D. no error

_____ **2.** That year, a Dutch ship <u>deliverred</u> 20 Africans to Jamestown, Virginia; the new arrivals were put to work, but not as slaves.

    F. deliverrd

    G. deliverd

    H. delivered

    J. no error

_____ **3.** These Africans had <u>sailed</u> to America as indentured servants, just as many Europeans did in those times.

    A. sayled

    B. saild

    C. sailled

    D. no error

_____ **4.** In early <u>colonyal</u> days, a form of contract labor called indentured servitude offered poor individuals a way to afford ship's passage to America.

    F. colonial

    G. colonyial

    H. colonal

    J. no error

_____ **5.** A large <u>majorrity</u> of indentured servants were German, English, and Scottish.

    A. majorty

    B. majority

    C. majorety

    D. no error

_____ **6.** They made contracts with ship's captains, who transported them free of charge and <u>lateer</u> sold the contracts to American colonists.

    F. latter

    G. later

    H. lator

    J. no error

_____ **7.** The term of a contract was <u>usualy</u> five to seven years; once the servant's term was over, he or she was a free colonist.

    A. usualley

    B. usualey

    C. usually

    D. no error

_____ **8.** Indentured servitude was technically "contract labor," but in all <u>faireness</u>, it was little better than slavery.

    F. fairrness

    G. fairness

    H. fairnness

    J. no error

_____ **9.** Despite <u>begining</u> their stay as servants, all of them—blacks and whites—had the right to earn their freedom and, afterward, own property.

    A. begininng

    B. begineing

    C. beginning

    D. no error

_____ **10.** For a lucky few, <u>acheiving</u> freedom could take as little as one year.

    F. achieving

    G. acheiveing

    H. achieveing

    J. no error

_____ **11.** <u>Haveing</u> come from Africa, Anthony Johnson, for example, arrived in indentured servitude in 1621.

    A. Having

    B. Haveeing

    C. Havinng

    D. no error

_____ **12.** He <u>laborred</u> for a Virginian colonist, and one year later, he was freed.

    F. labered

    G. labord

    H. labored

    J. no error

_____ **13.** Johnson prospered, and around 30 years later he imported five <u>serveants</u> of his own.

    A. serviants

    B. servents

    C. servants

    D. no error

_____ **14.** The ability of indentured blacks to earn freedom and own property had a direct impact on the structure of early colonial <u>society</u>.

    F. soceity

    G. societty

    H. socity

    J. no error

_____ **15.** <u>Specificaly</u>, a class of free blacks, though small, was able to form and grow in Virginia.

    A. Specificlly

    B. Specifically

    C. Specificly

    D. no error

Parts of Speech, Punctuation, Capitalization, and Spelling

PART 1 _____

Directions: Look at the item with the same number as the underlined part. Circle the letter of the best replacement for the underlined part. If the current part is best, then circle *A* or *F* for *NO CHANGE*.

During the 1950s and 60s, artists developed an art style
                                 1
called pop art (short for popular art). In this interesting art form, painters, sculptors, and other kinds of artists drew their inspiration from popular

_____ **1. A.** NO CHANGE
    B. '60s
    C. 60's
    D. 60s'

culture comic strips, advertisements, billboards, and
  2
other images related to brand names showed

_____ **2. F.** NO CHANGE
    G. culture, comic
    H. culture Comic
    J. culture. Comic

up artistic creations.
    3

_____ **3. A.** NO CHANGE
    B. up artistically creations
    C. up, artistic creations
    D. up in artistic creations

For example, roy lichtenstein's *Nurse,* an oil and magna
                  4
on canvas,

_____ **4. F.** NO CHANGE
    G. roy lichtensteins
    H. Roy Lichtenstein's
    J. roy Lichtenstein's

shows a woman nurse's head and shoulders in cartoon style;
          5

_____ **5. A.** NO CHANGE
    B. style,
    C. style!
    D. style:

the effect is that of being a newspaper cliping.
                            6

_____ **6. F.** NO CHANGE
    G. clipping
    H. clipeing
    J. clipinng

Many pop art pieces feature representations of <u>plainly,</u>
₇
everyday objects such as pencils, clothespins, and telephones. Claes Oldenburg's *Clothespin,*

_____ **7.** **A.** NO CHANGE
B. planely,
C. plane,
D. plain,

a 45-foot-high steel sculpture, is a clothespin in <u>pro-portions that are gigantic</u>.
₈

_____ **8.** **F.** NO CHANGE
G. gigantically proportions
H. gigantic proportions
J. proportions that are huge

<u>Overall</u>, the pop art movement helped to expand
₉

_____ **9.** **A.** NO CHANGE
B. overall,
C. Overall:
D. Overall;

<u>artists</u> subject matter.
₁₀

_____ **10.** **F.** NO CHANGE
G. artists's
H. artist's
J. artists'

PART 2

Directions: In each item, certain parts are underlined and labeled. Circle the letter of the underlined part that contains an error. If the item has no error, circle *E* for *No error*.

_____ **11.** Timothy <u>was exhausted</u> after football practice, <u>and</u> he helped his <u>father</u> rake the
                   A   **B**   **C**
      <u>leaves</u> before resting. <u>No error</u>
      D   **E**

_____ **12.** <u>Twelve</u> members of the choir wore <u>clean</u>, pressed <u>robes</u>; two members wore
      A   **B**   **C**
      crushed, <u>wrinkley</u> robes. <u>No error</u>
            D   **E**

_____ **13.** <u>Ick!</u> Why <u>didn't</u> I notice I used an old, moldy <u>piece</u> of cheese to make this <u>sandwich?</u>
      A   **B**   **C**   **D**
      <u>No error</u>
      E

_____ **14.** The administrators at <u>Ginnie's</u> school <u>are considered</u> the removal of all sugary or
                            A   **B**
      <u>fatty</u> snacks from vending machines on school <u>property</u>. <u>No error</u>
      C   **D**   **E**

_____ **15.** <u>Grapes</u> and <u>peaches</u> were in season, and <u>it was</u> on sale <u>at the market</u>. <u>No error</u>
           A   **B**   **C**   **D**   **E**

_____ **16.** I told the <u>officer</u> I didn't know what the speed limit was on that <u>road,</u> but he <u>said,</u>
                 A   **B**   **C**

"Ignorance is no excuse for <u>speeding</u>." <u>No error</u>
                         D   **E**

_____ **17.** Speaking <u>hypothetical</u>, the old, boarded up lighthouse <u>near</u> the rocks <u>could be</u>
                 A   **B**   **C**

transformed into a <u>really</u> unique home. <u>No error</u>
                D   **E**

_____ **18.** My <u>aunt</u> Florence spoke <u>forcfully</u> when she <u>said,</u> "Do not stick your finger in the
          A   **B**   **C**

frosting on this <u>cake!</u>" <u>No error</u>
               D   **E**

_____ **19.** From your <u>studies</u> in <u>history,</u> do you remember who first used the <u>phrase</u> "manifest
                A   **B**   **C**

destiny?" <u>No error</u>
   D   **E**

_____ **20.** I read "<u>Stopping</u> by Woods <u>on a</u> Snowy Evening" for the first time in sixth grade, and
              A   **B**

I fell in love with this <u>beautiful</u> poem. <u>No error</u>
C   **D**   **E**

Glossary

adjective	Part of speech used to modify a noun or a pronoun.
adverb	Part of speech used to modify a verb, an adjective, or another adverb.
antecedent	The word or word group to which a pronoun refers.
apostrophe	Punctuation mark used to form contractions and possessives.
article	A special group of adjectives. The articles are *a*, *an*, and *the*.
comma	Punctuation mark used to separate items in a series, among other tasks.
conjunction	Part of speech used to link words, phrases, clauses, or sentences.
dialogue	Written conversation in a story.
direct object	A noun that receives the action of a verb.
exclamation point	Punctuation mark used to end expressions of strong feeling.
indirect object	A noun that is indirectly affected by the action of the verb.
interjection	Part of speech used to express sudden, strong feeling. It usually stands alone before a sentence.
italics	Slanted type used to punctuate titles of long works. Handwriting uses underlining instead of italics.
noun	Part of speech that names a person, place, thing, or idea.
object of a preposition	The noun that a preposition links to another word in the sentence.
period	Punctuation mark used to end statements, polite requests, and commands.
predicate	The part of a sentence that says something about the subject.
preposition	Part of speech that shows the relationship between its object(s) and another word in the sentence.
pronoun	Part of speech that takes the place of a noun in a sentence.
question mark	Punctuation mark used to end inquiries.
quotation marks	Punctuation marks used to enclose a speaker's exact words and titles of short works.
subject	The word or word group about which the predicate says something.
verb	Part of speech that expresses action or links the subject to another word in the sentence.

Index

A

Abbreviations, capitalization of, 175
Abstract nouns, 39
Action verbs, 20, 21–23, 47, 50
Adjectives, 77, 80, 219
  articles as, 77, 219
  forming, from nouns, 83
  forming adverbs from, 97
  placement of, 79
  predicate, 88
  proper, 82–83, 84, 175
  recognizing, 99–100
  redundant, 86
Adverbs, 92, 219
  conjunctive, 149
  distinguishing from prepositions, 109
  forming from adjectives, 97
  not as, 29
  placement of, 93, 95
  recognizing, 99–100
  uses of, 92, 94, 95
Agreement, pronoun-antecedent, 61–62
Antecedents, 56, 58, 219
  agreement with pronouns, 61–62
Apostrophes, 153, 219
  in contractions, 29, 64, 153, 205
  to form possessives, 153, 205
Articles *(a, an, the)*, 77, 219
Auxiliary verbs. *See* Helping verbs

B

be verbs, 47

C

Capitalization, 174–175
  of abbreviations, 175
  of brand names, 178
  in dialogue, 175
  of family relationships, 179
  of first word and nouns in salutation, 176
  of first word in closing, 176
  of first word of a quotation, 174
  of first word of a sentence, 174
  of geographical names, 177
  of *I*, 174
  of names of planets, satellites, stars, and constellations, 178
  of particular persons, 177
  of political parties, nations, governmental bodies, 177
  of proper adjectives, 82–83, 175
  of proper nouns, 41, 42, 175–176
  of religious terms, 178
  of school subjects, 179
  of sections of the country, 179
  of titles

of organizations, companies, and buildings, 177
of persons showing office, rank, profession, 177
of publications, 176
Closing, capitalization of first words in, 176
Colons, 148
  after salutation in letter, 151
  to call attention to what follows, 150–151
  with quotation marks, 158
Commas, 144, 219
  after expressions introducing quotations, 156
  after interjections, 122
  after introductory words/word groups, 144
  with compound verbs, 33
  before coordinating conjunctions, 144
  with direct quotations, 156
  with quotation marks, 157
  in series, 144
  to set off interrupting words and expressions, 144
  speech patterns and, 146
Common nouns, 41, 42, 75
Complements, 87, 90
  predicate, 88
  subject, 88
Complete subjects, 5, 6, 8, 9
Compound direct objects, 48
Compound indirect objects, 63
Compound nouns, 40
Compound objects, 63
Compound sentences, 119
Compound subjects, 2, 12, 37, 63
Compound verbs, 32–33, 34, 37
Conciseness in writing, 28, 85, 99
Concrete nouns, 39
Conjunctions, 116, 125, 219
  in combining sentences, 119
  coordinating, 144, 148
  uses of, 116, 117
Conjunctive adverbs, 149
Contractions, 29, 30, 31, 64, 168
  apostrophes in, 29, 64, 153
  pronouns in, 64
  verbs in, 29
Coordinating conjunctions, 144, 148

D

Dialogue, 219
  capitalization in, 175
  incomplete sentences in, 174
  quotation marks in, 167
Dictionaries for spelling, 195
Direct objects, 46, 50, 54, 219
  compound, 48
  nouns as, 46–47

Direct quotations, 156
  commas with, 156

E

End punctuation, 142–143
ESL Focus
  contractions, 31
  forming adjectives from nouns, 83
  placement of adjectives, 79
  placement of adverbs, 93, 95
  subject of a sentence, 5
  titles, 178
Exclamation points, 219
  after interjections, 122
  as end punctuation, 142
  with quotation marks, 159

G

Gender, pronoun-antecedent agreement in, 61–62
Grammar, 1

H

Helping verbs, 25–26

I

I, capitalization of, 174
Idioms, 135
Imperative sentences, 4
  you as understood in, 4, 5
Indirect objects, 50, 51, 54, 219
  compound, 51, 63
  nouns as, 50, 51
Indirect quotations, 156
Interjections, 122, 125, 219
  common, 122
  punctuation with, 122
Italics, 219
  for titles of longer works, 161

L

Letters
  capitalization of first word and nouns in salutation, 176
  capitalization of first word in closing, 176
  colons after salutation in, 151
Linking verbs, 20, 21–23, 47, 87, 88

M

Main verbs, 25
Mnemonic devices, 211
Modifiers. *See* Adjectives; Adverbs

N

Nouns, 38, 219
  abstract, 39
  common, 41, 42, 75
  compound, 40

Nouns (continued)
concrete, 39
as direct objects, 46–47
forming adjectives from, 83
as indirect objects, 50, 51
plural, 197, 198–199, 200, 202, 203, 204
predicate, 89, 90
proper, 41, 42, 75, 175–176
singular, 197
Number, pronoun-antecedent agreement in, 61–62

O

Objects
compound, 63
direct, 46–47
indirect, 50, 51, 54
of the preposition, 109–110, 111, 219

P

Parallel structure, 117
Parts of speech, 1. *See also specific*
Periods, 219
as end punctuation, 142
with quotation marks, 157
Personal pronouns, 59–60, 61
Phrases
prepositional, 110–111, 113
transitional, 149
verb, 25
Plural nouns, forming, 197, 198–199, 200, 202, 203, 204
Possessive nouns, apostrophes in, 153
Possessive pronouns, 65
Predicate adjectives, 89, 90
Predicate complements, 88
Predicate nouns, 89, 90
Predicates, 2, 13–14, 17, 219
position of, in sentence, 14–15
Preposition(s), 107, 125, 219
common, 107
distinguishing from adverbs, 109
ending sentences with, 114
objects of, 109–110
Prepositional phrases, 110–111, 113
Pronouns, 56, 58, 75, 219
agreement with antecedents, 61–62
in combinations, 63
in contractions, 64
importance of, 56
indefinite, 153
personal, 59–60
possessive, 65

Proper adjectives, 82–83, 84
capitalization of, 82–83, 175
Proper nouns, 41, 42, 75
capitalization of, 175–176
Punctuation, 141
See also specific
end, 142–143

Q

Question marks, 219
as end punctuation, 142
with quotation marks, 159
Questions
verb phrases in, 28
word order in, 26–27
Quotation(s)
capitalization of first word of, 174
commas after expressions introducing, 156
direct, 156
indirect, 156
Quotation marks, 156, 219
in dialogue, 167
to enclose speaker's exact words, 156
other marks of punctuation with, 157, 158, 159
for titles of short works, 161

S

Salutation
capitalization of first word and nouns in, 176
colon after, 151
Semicolons
in forming compound sentences, 148–149
with quotation marks, 158
in series, 149
Sentences
capitalization of first word of, 174
compound, 119
ending, with prepositions, 114
imperative, 4
parallel structure in, 117
parts of, 2, 13
simple, 119
Simple sentences, 8, 119
Simple subjects, 5, 6
Singular nouns, 197
Spanish
subject of a sentence in, 5
word order in, 135
Spelling, 189
rules of

for adding *ly* or *ness,* 193
in adding prefixes, 190–191
doubling of final consonant, 194
for *ie* and *ei,* 190
for words ending in silent *e,* 191
for words ending in *y,* 192
using dictionary for, 195
Standard English, contractions in, 31
Subject complements, 88
Subjects, 2–5, 13, 219
complete, 5, 6, 8, 9
compound, 2, 12, 37, 63
position in sentence, 3
simple, 5, 6, 8
Suffixes, 83, 84

T

the, need for, in titles, 178
Thesaurus, 75
Titles
capitalization of, 176
italics for longer works, 161
need for *the* in, 178
quotation marks for short works, 161
Transitional phrases, 149
Typos, 212

U

Underlining. *See* Italics

V

Verb(s), 18, 75, 219
action, 20, 21–23, 47, 50
compound, 32–33, 34, 37
in contractions, 29
helping, 25–26
linking, 20, 21–23, 47, 87, 88
main, 25
Verb phrases, 21, 25
in questions, 28

W

Wordiness in writing, 28, 85, 114
Words
nouns as verbs, 73
order of, in questions, 26–27
Writing
conciseness in, 28, 85, 99
redundancy in, 86
wordiness in, 28, 85, 114

Y

You, as understood subject in imperative sentences, 4, 5

1) Verb. Canadian red foxes <u>have moved</u> north." What is the subject?"

Notes

1. Verb: NOT is not part of the verb!
   I <u>could go</u> to the party. vs. I <u>could</u> not <u>go</u> to the party.